everyday
chocolate

This edition published in 2010
LOVE FOOD is an imprint of Parragon Books Ltd

Parragon
Queen Street House
4 Queen Street
Bath BA1 1HE, UK

ISBN: 978-1-4054-9395-6

Printed in China

Designed by Terry Jeavons & Company

Notes for the Reader
This book uses both metric and imperial measurements. Follow the same units of measurement throughout; do not mix metric and imperial. All spoon measurements are level: teaspoons are assumed to be 5 ml, and tablespoons are assumed to be 15 ml. Unless otherwise stated, milk is assumed to be full fat, eggs and individual vegetables are medium, and pepper is freshly ground black pepper.

The times given are an approximate guide only. Preparation times differ according to the techniques used by different people and the cooking times may also vary from those given. Optional ingredients, variations or serving suggestions have not been included in the calculations.

Recipes using raw or very lightly cooked eggs should be avoided by infants, the elderly, pregnant women, convalescents and anyone suffering from an illness. Pregnant and breastfeeding women are advised to avoid eating peanuts and peanut products. Sufferers from nut allergies should be aware that some of the ready-made ingredients used in the recipes in this book may contain nuts. Always check the packaging before use.

everyday chocolate

introduction

The very word 'chocolate' almost has a magic about it and those who love it will agree unanimously that the taste is quite definitely magical.

The remarkable story of chocolate dates back to the 7th century, when the cocoa tree, *Theobroma cacao*, was cultivated by the Maya of Central America. This ancient civilization established a flourishing trade, even using the cocoa bean as currency. The explorer Christopher Columbus took the cocoa bean to Spain in 1502, and Hernán Cortés, who conquered Mexico for Spain, soon afterwards got an idea of what to do with this curious object when the Aztec Emperor Montezuma introduced

him to *xocotlatl*, a drink made of crushed, roasted cocoa beans and cold water. This bitter-tasting brew soon evolved into something more pleasant when it was served hot with a flavouring of vanilla, spices, honey and sugar.

By the late 17th century, Europe and beyond had fallen under the spell of the 'hot chocolate' drink, but it is a 19th-century Dutch chemist, Coenraad Van Houten, whom we have to thank for chocolate that we can eat. This veritable hero invented a method of producing pure cocoa butter and a hard 'cake' that could be milled to produce cocoa 'powder' for flavouring. Within a very short time, the chocolate industry was founded, going from strength to strength as different countries began to produce smooth, melt-in-the-mouth chocolate bars.

Today – to our delight – there is no end to the creative ways in which chocolate is used in cooking. Puddings, cakes, biscuits, chilled desserts, ice creams – they all seem to have a little extra appeal when they include chocolate. Even the original concept, hot chocolate, has been miraculously transformed into an exceptionally good cheesecake.

If you are one of the world's many chocoholics, you'll love this book. Just dip in and be indulgent!

puddings

In this chapter you'll find a few of the favourite traditional chocolate pudding recipes. You'll also find several traditional recipes given a modern twist by transforming them with chocolate! For example, you might have tried a classic lemon meringue pie, but have you thought of trying a rich, creamy chocolate filling beneath that melting meringue topping? Adding a touch of cocoa to make a Pecan Pie or Bread Pudding even more delectable? Or finishing off a special dinner party with a superb flourish – a stylish Italian Zabaglione, but with chocolate?

Chocolate marries very successfully with fruit, as you'll soon discover. Fold your favourite fruits inside a chocolate crêpe, add a handful of chocolate chips to a fruit crumble topping, or dunk chilled fruit into a warm chocolate fondue. Make the most of the brief season for blueberries and blackberries with flans, pies and possibly the most delicious chocolate steamed pudding you'll ever taste, served with a rum syrup.

An important tip to bear in mind when making any recipe that includes chocolate is to use a top-quality product with the highest cocoa butter content you can find – around 70 per cent – as this gives a far superior taste. It might cost a little more but you will get a really excellent result.

fine chocolate tart

ingredients

SERVES 6

pastry

150 g/5 oz plain flour
2 tsp cocoa powder
2 tsp icing sugar
pinch of salt
50 g/1¾ oz cold butter, cut into pieces
1 egg yolk
ice-cold water

ganache filling

200 g/7 oz plain chocolate with 70% cocoa solids
2 tbsp unsalted butter, softened
250 ml/9 fl oz double cream
1 tsp dark rum (optional)
chocolate curls, to serve

method

1 Lightly grease a 22-cm/9-inch loose-based fluted tart tin. Sift the flour, cocoa, icing sugar and salt into a food processor, add the butter and process until the mixture resembles fine breadcrumbs. Tip the mixture into a large bowl, add the egg yolk, and add just enough ice-cold water to bring the pastry together. Turn out onto a work surface dusted with more flour and cocoa and roll out the pastry about 7.5 cm/3 inches larger than the tin. Carefully lift the pastry into the tin and press to fit. Roll the rolling pin over the tin to neaten the edges and trim the excess pastry. Fit a piece of baking parchment into the tart shell, fill with baking beans, and chill in the refrigerator for 30 minutes.

2 Remove the pastry case from the refrigerator and bake in a preheated oven, 190°C/375°F, for 15 minutes, then remove the beans and paper and bake for a further 5 minutes.

3 To make the ganache filling, chop the chocolate and put in a bowl with the softened butter. Bring the cream to the boil, then pour onto the chocolate, stirring well, add the rum (if using) and continue stirring to make sure the chocolate is melted completely. Pour into the pastry case and chill for 3 hours. Serve decorated with chocolate curls.

white chocolate & cardamom tart

ingredients

SERVES 6

pastry

150 g/5 oz plain flour
pinch of salt
75 g/2 1/2 oz cold butter, cut into pieces
cold water

filling

seeds of 8 cardamom pods
350 g/12 oz white chocolate, chopped into small pieces
2 pieces or 6 g/1/4 oz fine leaf gelatine
cold water
425 ml/15 fl oz whipping cream

shavings of white chocolate, to decorate

method

1 Sift the flour and salt into a food processor, add the butter and process until the mixture resembles fine breadcrumbs. Tip into a large bowl and add just enough cold water to bring the pastry together. Lightly grease a 22-cm/9-inch loose-based fluted tart tin. Turn out the pastry onto a lightly floured work surface and roll out to 7.5 cm/3 inches larger than the tin. Carefully lift the pastry into the tin and press to fit. Roll the rolling pin over the tin to trim the excess pastry. Fit a piece of baking parchment into the tart shell and fill with baking beans.

2 Chill for 30 minutes, then remove from the refrigerator and bake blind for 15 minutes in a preheated oven, 190°C/375°F. Remove the beans and paper and bake for a further 10 minutes. Set aside to cool completely.

3 Crush the cardamom seeds until powdery and put in a large bowl with the chocolate. Soak the gelatine in a little cold water in a heatproof bowl for 5 minutes, then stir over a saucepan of simmering water until dissolved. At the same time, in a separate pan, heat the cream until just boiling, then pour over the chocolate, whisking until the chocolate has melted. Add the gelatine and stir the mixture until smooth. Allow to cool, then pour into the tart shell and chill for at least 3 hours.

chocolate fudge tart

ingredients

SERVES 6–8

flour, for sprinkling
350 g/12 oz ready-made shortcrust pastry
icing sugar, for dusting

filling

140 g/5 oz plain chocolate, finely chopped
175 g/6 oz butter, diced
350 g/12 oz golden granulated sugar
100 g/3½ oz plain flour
½ tsp vanilla essence
6 eggs, beaten

to decorate

150 ml/5 fl oz whipped cream
ground cinnamon

method

1 Roll out the pastry on a lightly floured work surface and use to line a 20-cm/8-inch deep loose-based tart tin. Prick the base lightly with a fork, then line with foil and fill with baking beans. Bake in a preheated oven, 200°C/400°F, for 12–15 minutes, or until the pastry no longer looks raw. Remove the beans and foil and bake for a further 10 minutes, or until the pastry is firm. Allow to cool. Reduce the oven temperature to 180°C/350°F.

2 To make the filling, place the chocolate and butter in a heatproof bowl and set over a saucepan of gently simmering water until melted. Stir until smooth, then remove from the heat and set aside to cool. Place the sugar, flour, vanilla essence and eggs in a separate bowl and whisk until well blended. Stir in the butter and chocolate mixture.

3 Pour the filling into the pastry case and bake in the oven for 50 minutes, or until the filling is just set. Transfer to a wire rack to cool completely. Dust with icing sugar before serving with whipped cream sprinkled lightly with cinnamon.

lemon & chocolate tart

ingredients

SERVES 8–10

100 g/3½ oz plain flour
25 g/1 oz cocoa powder
75 g/2¾ oz butter
25 g/1 oz ground almonds
50 g/1¾ oz golden caster sugar
1 egg, beaten
chocolate curls, to decorate

filling

4 eggs
1 egg yolk
200 g/7 oz golden caster sugar
150 ml/5 fl oz double cream
grated rind and juice of 2 lemons

method

1 Sift the flour and cocoa powder into a food processor. Add the butter, almonds, sugar and egg and process until the mixture forms a ball. Gather the pastry together and press into a flattened ball. Place in the centre of a 22-cm/8½-inch loose-based tart tin and press evenly over the bottom of the tin with your fingers, then work the pastry up the sides with your thumbs. Allow any excess pastry to go over the edge. Cover and chill for 30 minutes.

2 Roll the rolling pin over the tin to trim the excess pastry. Prick the pastry base lightly with a fork, then line with baking parchment and fill with baking beans. Bake in a preheated oven, 200°C/400°F, for 12–15 minutes, or until the pastry no longer looks raw. Remove the beans and paper, return to the oven and bake for 10 minutes, or until the pastry is firm. Allow to cool. Reduce the oven temperature to 150°C/300°F.

3 To make the filling, whisk the whole eggs, egg yolk and sugar together until smooth. Add the cream and whisk again, then stir in the lemon rind and juice. Pour the filling into the pastry case and bake for 50 minutes, or until just set. When the tart is cooked, remove the tart ring and allow to cool. Decorate with chocolate curls before serving.

blackberry chocolate flan

ingredients

SERVES 6

pastry

175 g/6 oz plain flour, plus extra for dusting
30 g/1 oz cocoa powder
55 g/2 oz icing sugar
pinch of salt
85 g/3 oz unsalted butter, cut into small pieces
1/2 egg yolk

filling

300 ml/10 fl oz double cream
175 g/6 oz blackberry jam
225 g/8 oz plain chocolate, broken into pieces
2 tbsp unsalted butter, cut into small pieces

sauce

675 g/1 lb 8 oz blackberries, plus extra for decoration
1 tbsp lemon juice
2 tbsp caster sugar
2 tbsp crème de cassis

method

1 To make the pastry, sift the flour, cocoa, icing sugar and salt into a mixing bowl and make a well in the centre. Place the butter and egg yolk in the well and gradually mix in the dry ingredients using a pastry blender. Knead lightly and form into a ball. Wrap the pastry and chill in the refrigerator for 1 hour.

2 Roll out the pastry on a lightly floured work surface and use to line a 30 x 10-cm/12 x 4-inch rectangular tart tin. Prick the base with a fork, line with baking parchment, and fill with baking beans. Bake in a preheated oven, 180°C/350°F, for 15 minutes. Remove the beans and paper and cook for a further 5 minutes. Set aside to cool.

3 To make the filling, place the cream and jam in a saucepan and bring to the boil over low heat. Remove from the heat and stir in the chocolate and then the butter until melted and smooth. Pour the mixture into the pastry case and set aside to cool.

4 To make the sauce, whiz the blackberries, lemon juice and caster sugar in a food processor until smooth. Strain through a nylon sieve into a bowl and stir in the cassis.

5 Transfer the flan to a serving plate. Arrange the remaining blackberries on top and brush with a little blackberry and liqueur sauce. Serve with the remaining sauce on the side.

boston cream pie

ingredients

SERVES 6

225 g/8 oz ready-made shortcrust pastry

filling

3 eggs
115 g/4 oz caster sugar
150 g/5 oz plain flour, plus extra for dusting
1 tbsp icing sugar
pinch of salt
1 tsp vanilla essence
400 ml/14 fl oz milk
150 ml/5 fl oz plain yogurt
150 g/5½ oz plain chocolate, broken into pieces
2 tbsp Kirsch

to decorate

150 ml/5 fl oz sour cream
225 g/8 oz plain chocolate shavings or caraque

method

1 Roll out the pastry and use to line a 23-cm/9-inch loose-based tart tin. Prick the base with a fork, line with baking parchment, and fill with baking beans. Bake in a preheated oven, 200°C/400°F, for 20 minutes. Remove the beans and paper and return the pastry case to the oven for a further 5 minutes. Remove from the oven and place on a wire rack to cool.

2 To make the filling, beat the eggs and caster sugar in a heatproof bowl until fluffy. Sift in the flour, icing sugar and salt. Stir in the vanilla essence.

3 Bring the milk and yogurt to the boil in a small saucepan and strain it over the egg mixture. Set the bowl over a saucepan of barely simmering water. Stir the custard until it coats the back of a spoon.

4 Gently heat the chocolate with the Kirsch in a separate small saucepan until the chocolate has melted. Stir into the custard. Remove from the heat and stand the bowl in cold water. Set aside to cool.

5 Pour the chocolate mixture into the pastry case. Spread the sour cream evenly over the chocolate and decorate with chocolate shavings or caraque.

chocolate meringue pie

ingredients

SERVES 6

225 g/8 oz plain chocolate digestive biscuits
4 tbsp butter

filling

3 egg yolks
4 tbsp caster sugar
4 tbsp cornflour
600 ml/1pint milk
100 g/3½ oz plain chocolate, melted

meringue

2 egg whites
100 g/3½ oz caster sugar
¼ tsp vanilla essence

method

1 Place the chocolate digestives in a plastic bag and crush with a rolling pin, then transfer to a large bowl. Place the butter in a small, heavy-based saucepan and heat gently until just melted, then stir it into the biscuit crumbs until well mixed. Press into the bottom and up the sides of a 23-cm/9-inch tart tin or dish.

2 To make the filling, place the egg yolks, caster sugar and cornflour in a large bowl and beat until they form a smooth paste, adding a little of the milk, if necessary. Place the milk in a small, heavy-based saucepan and heat gently until almost boiling, then slowly pour it onto the egg mixture, whisking well.

3 Return the mixture to the pan and cook gently, whisking, until thick. Remove from the heat. Whisk in the melted chocolate, then pour it onto the biscuit base.

4 To make the meringue, whisk the egg whites in a large, spotlessly clean, greasefree bowl until soft peaks form. Gradually whisk in two-thirds of the sugar until the mixture is stiff and glossy. Fold in the remaining sugar and vanilla essence.

5 Spread the meringue over the filling, swirling the surface with the back of a spoon to give it an attractive finish. Bake in the centre of a preheated oven, 160°C/375°F, for 30 minutes, or until golden. Serve hot or just warm.

chocolate chiffon pie

ingredients

SERVES 8

nut base

225 g/8 oz shelled Brazil nuts
4 tbsp granulated sugar
4 tsp melted butter

filling

225 ml/8 fl oz milk
2 tsp powdered gelatine
115 g/4 oz caster sugar
2 eggs, separated
225 g/8 oz plain chocolate, roughly chopped
1 tsp vanilla essence
150 ml/5 fl oz double cream
2 tbsp chopped Brazil nuts, to decorate

method

1 Process the whole Brazil nuts in a food processor until finely ground. Add the granulated sugar and melted butter and process briefly to combine. Tip the mixture into a 23-cm/9-inch round tart tin and press it onto the base and sides with a spoon. Bake in a preheated oven, 200°C/ 400°F, for 8–10 minutes, or until light golden brown. Set aside to cool.

2 Pour the milk into a heatproof bowl and sprinkle over the gelatine. Leave it to soften for 2 minutes, then set over a saucepan of gently simmering water. Stir in half of the caster sugar, both the egg yolks and all the chocolate. Stir constantly over low heat for 4–5 minutes until the gelatine has dissolved and the chocolate has melted. Remove from the heat and beat until smooth. Stir in the vanilla essence, cover and chill in the refrigerator for 45–60 minutes until starting to set.

3 Whip the cream until stiff, then fold all but 3 tablespoons into the chocolate mixture. Whisk the egg whites in a clean, greasefree bowl until soft peaks form. Add 2 teaspoons of the remaining sugar and whisk until stiff peaks form. Fold in the remaining sugar, then fold the egg whites into the chocolate mixture. Pour the filling into the pastry case and chill in the refrigerator for 3 hours. Decorate the pie with the remaining whipped cream and the chopped nuts before serving.

pecan & chocolate pie

ingredients

SERVES 6–8

pastry

175 g/6 oz plain flour, plus extra for dusting

100 g/3½ oz butter, diced

1 tbsp golden caster sugar

1 egg yolk, beaten with 1 tbsp water

filling

55 g/2 oz butter

3 tbsp cocoa powder

225 ml/8 fl oz golden syrup

3 eggs

70 g/2½ oz firmly packed dark brown sugar

175 g/6 oz shelled pecan nuts, chopped

to serve

whipped cream

ground cinnamon, for dusting

method

1 To make the pastry, sift the flour into a large bowl. Rub in the butter until the mixture resembles fine breadcrumbs, then stir in the caster sugar. Stir in the beaten egg yolk. Knead lightly to form a firm dough, cover with clingfilm and chill in the refrigerator for 1½ hours. Roll out the chilled pastry on a lightly floured work surface and use it to line a 20-cm/8-inch tart tin.

2 To make the filling, place the butter in a small, heavy-based saucepan and heat gently until melted. Sift in the cocoa and stir in the syrup. Place the eggs and sugar in a large bowl and beat together. Add the syrup mixture and the chopped pecan nuts and stir. Pour the mixture into the prepared pastry case.

3 Place the pie on a preheated baking sheet and bake in a preheated oven, 190°C/375°F, for 35–40 minutes, or until the filling is just set. Leave it to cool slightly and serve warm with a spoonful of whipped cream, dusted with ground cinnamon.

mississippi mud pie

ingredients

SERVES 8

pastry

225 g/8 oz plain flour, plus extra for dusting
2 tbsp cocoa powder
150 g/5½ oz butter
2 tbsp caster sugar
1–2 tbsp cold water

filling

175 g/6 oz butter
350 g/12 oz brown sugar
4 eggs, lightly beaten
4 tbsp cocoa powder, sifted
150 g/5½ oz plain chocolate
300 ml/10 fl oz single cream
1 tsp chocolate extract

to decorate

425 ml/15 fl oz double cream, whipped
chocolate flakes and curls

method

1 To make the pastry, sift the flour and cocoa into a mixing bowl. Rub in the butter with the fingertips until the mixture resembles fine breadcrumbs. Stir in the sugar and enough cold water to mix to a soft dough. Wrap the dough and chill in the refrigerator for 15 minutes.

2 Roll out the pastry on a lightly floured work surface and use to line a 23-cm/9-inch loose-based tart tin or ceramic pie dish. Line with baking parchment and fill with baking beans. Bake in a preheated oven, 190°C/375°F, for 15 minutes. Remove from the oven and take out the beans and parchment. Bake the pastry case for a further 10 minutes.

3 To make the filling, beat the butter and sugar together in a bowl and gradually beat in the eggs with the cocoa. Melt the chocolate and beat it into the mixture with the single cream and the chocolate extract.

4 Reduce the oven temperature to 160°C/325°F. Pour the mixture into the pastry case and bake for 45 minutes, or until the filling has set gently.

5 Allow the mud pie to cool completely, then transfer it to a serving plate, if you like. Cover with the whipped cream. Decorate the pie with chocolate flakes and curls and then chill until ready to serve.

chocolate crumble pie

ingredients

SERVES 8

pastry

200 g/7 oz plain flour
1 tsp baking powder
115 g/4 oz unsalted butter, cut into small pieces
25 g/1 oz caster sugar
1 egg yolk
1–2 tsp cold water

filling

150 ml/5 fl oz double cream
150 ml/5 fl oz milk
225 g/8 oz plain chocolate, chopped
2 eggs

crumble topping

100 g/3½ oz brown sugar
85 g/3 oz toasted pecan nuts
115 g/4 oz plain chocolate
85 g/3 oz amaretti biscuits
1 tsp cocoa powder

method

1 To make the pastry, sift the flour and baking powder into a large bowl, rub in the butter, and stir in the sugar, then add the egg and a little water to bring the pastry together. Turn the pastry out and knead briefly. Wrap the pastry and chill in the refrigerator for 30 minutes.

2 Preheat the oven to 190°C/375°F. Roll out the pastry and use to line a 23-cm/9-inch loose-based tart tin. Prick the pastry case with a fork. Line with baking parchment and fill with baking beans. Bake in the oven for 15 minutes. Remove from the oven and take out the beans and parchment. Reduce the oven temperature to 180°C/350°F.

3 Bring the cream and milk to the boil in a saucepan, remove from the heat, and add the chocolate. Stir until melted and smooth. Beat the eggs and add to the chocolate mixture, mix thoroughly and pour into the shell. Bake for 15 minutes, remove from the oven and leave it to rest for 1 hour.

4 When you are ready to serve the pie, place the topping ingredients in the food processor and pulse to chop. (If you do not have a processor, place the sugar in a large bowl, chop the nuts and chocolate with a large knife, and crush the biscuits, then add to the bowl with the cocoa and mix well.) Sprinkle over the pie, then serve it in slices.

chocolate blueberry pies

ingredients

MAKES 10

pastry

200 g/7 oz plain flour
55 g/2oz cocoa powder
55 g/2oz caster sugar
pinch of salt
125 g/4½ oz butter, cut into small pieces
1 egg yolk
1–2 tbsp cold water

sauce

200 g/6 oz blueberries
2 tbsp crème de cassis
10 g/½ oz icing sugar, sifted

filling

140 g/5 oz plain chocolate
225 ml/7½ fl oz double cream
150 ml/5 fl oz sour cream

method

1 To make the pastry, place the flour, cocoa, sugar and salt in a large bowl and rub in the butter until the mixture resembles breadcrumbs. Add the egg and a little cold water to form a dough. Wrap the dough and chill in the refrigerator for 30 minutes.

2 Remove the pastry from the refrigerator and roll out. Use to line 10 x 10-cm/4-inch tart tins. Freeze for 30 minutes. Preheat the oven to 180°C/350°F. Bake the pastry cases in the oven for 15–20 minutes. Set aside to cool.

3 To make the sauce, place the blueberries, cassis and icing sugar in a saucepan and warm through so that the berries become shiny but do not burst. Set aside to cool.

4 To make the filling, melt the chocolate in a heatproof bowl set over a saucepan of simmering water, then cool slightly. Whip the cream until stiff and fold in the sour cream and chocolate.

5 Remove the pastry cases to a serving plate and divide the chocolate filling between them, smoothing the surface with a spatula, then top with the blueberries.

hot chocolate cheesecake

ingredients

SERVES 8

butter, for greasing

pastry

150 g/5½ oz plain flour
2 tbsp cocoa powder
75 g/2¾ oz butter, diced
2 tbsp golden caster sugar
25 g/1 oz ground almonds
1 egg yolk
icing sugar, for dusting

filling

2 eggs, separated
75 g/2¾ oz golden caster sugar
350 g/12 oz cream cheese
40 g/1½ oz ground almonds
150 ml/5 fl oz double cream
25 g/1 oz cocoa powder, sifted
1 tsp vanilla essence

method

1 To make the pastry, sift the flour and cocoa powder into a bowl. Add the butter and rub it in until the mixture resembles fine breadcrumbs. Stir in the sugar and almonds. Add the egg yolk and enough water to make a soft dough. Roll out on a lightly floured work surface and use to line a 20-cm/8-inch loose-based cake tin greased with butter. Chill in the refrigerator while preparing the filling.

2 To make the filling, place the egg yolks and caster sugar in a large bowl and whisk together until thick and pale. Whisk in the cheese, almonds, cream, cocoa and vanilla essence until blended.

3 Place the egg whites in a clean, greasefree bowl and whisk until stiff but not dry. Stir a little of the whisked egg whites into the cheese mixture, then fold in the remainder. Pour into the pastry case. Bake in a preheated oven, 160°C/325°F, for 1½ hours, or until risen and just firm to the touch. Remove from the tin and dust with icing sugar.

chocolate bread pudding

ingredients

SERVES 4

6 thick slices white bread, crusts removed
450 ml/16 fl oz milk
175 ml/6 fl oz canned evaporated milk
2 tbsp cocoa powder
2 eggs
2 tbsp brown sugar
1 tsp vanilla essence
icing sugar, for dusting

hot fudge sauce

55 g/2 oz plain chocolate, broken into pieces
1 tbsp cocoa powder
2 tbsp golden syrup
55 g/2 oz butter or margarine
2 tbsp brown sugar
150 ml/5 fl oz milk
1 tbsp cornflour

method

1 Grease a shallow ovenproof dish. Cut the bread into squares and layer them in the dish.

2 Put the milk, evaporated milk and cocoa powder in a saucepan and heat gently, stirring occasionally, until the mixture is lukewarm. Whisk the eggs, sugar and vanilla essence together. Add the warm milk mixture and beat well.

3 Pour into the prepared dish, making sure that all the bread is completely covered. Cover the dish with clingfilm and chill in the refrigerator for 1–2 hours, then bake in a preheated oven 180°C/350°F, for 35–40 minutes, until set. Stand for 5 minutes.

4 To make the sauce, put all the ingredients into a saucepan and heat gently, stirring constantly until smooth.

5 Dust the chocolate bread pudding with icing sugar and serve immediately with the hot fudge sauce.

saucy chocolate pudding

ingredients

SERVES 4–6

85 g/3 oz butter, softened, plus extra for greasing
55 g/2 oz self-raising flour
25 g/1 oz cocoa powder
1 tsp ground cinnamon
115 g/4 oz golden caster sugar
1 egg
2 tbsp dark brown sugar
55 g/2 oz shelled pecan nuts, chopped
300 ml/10 fl oz hot black coffee
icing sugar, for dusting
whipped cream, to serve

method

1 Grease a shallow 1.2-litre/2¾-pint ovenproof dish with a little butter. Sift the flour, cocoa powder and cinnamon into a large bowl. Add the butter, 85 g/3 oz of the caster sugar and the egg and beat together until the mixture is well blended. Turn into the prepared dish and sprinkle with the dark brown sugar and the pecan nuts.

2 Pour the coffee into a large jug, stir in the remaining caster sugar until dissolved and carefully pour over the pudding.

3 Bake in a preheated oven, 160°C/325°F, for 50–60 minutes, or until firm to the touch in the centre. Dust with a little icing sugar and serve with whipped cream.

chocolate fruit crumble

ingredients

SERVES 4

400 g/14 oz canned apricots, in natural juice
450 g/1 lb cooking apples, peeled and thickly sliced
6 tbsp butter, plus extra for greasing
100 g/3½ oz plain flour
50 g/1¾ oz rolled oats
4 tbsp caster sugar
100 g/3½ oz chocolate chips

method

1 Drain the apricots, reserving 4 tablespoons of the juice. Place the apples and apricots in a greased ovenproof dish with the reserved apricot juice and toss to mix thoroughly.

2 Sift the flour into a large bowl. Cut the butter into small cubes and rub it in with your fingertips until the mixture resembles fine breadcrumbs. Stir in the rolled oats, caster sugar and chocolate chips.

3 Sprinkle the crumble mixture over the apples and apricots and level the top roughly. Do not press the crumble down onto the fruit. Bake in a preheated oven, 350°F/180°C, for 40–45 minutes, or until the topping is golden. Serve the crumble hot or cold.

blueberry chocolate pudding with rum syrup

ingredients

SERVES 4

115 g/4 oz butter, softened, plus extra for greasing
115 g/4 oz soft brown sugar
2 eggs
150 g/5½ oz plain flour
½ tsp baking powder
2 tbsp cocoa powder
114 g/4 oz blueberries
whole blueberries, to decorate

rum syrup

120 g/4 oz plain chocolate, chopped
2 tbsp maple syrup
1 tbsp unsalted butter
1 tbsp rum

method

1 Grease a large pudding basin. Heat water to a depth of 7.5–10 cm/3–4 inches in a large saucepan over low heat until simmering.

2 Put the butter, sugar, eggs, flour, baking powder and cocoa powder into a large bowl and beat together until thoroughly mixed. Stir in the blueberries. Spoon the mixture into the prepared basin and cover tightly with two layers of foil. Carefully place the basin in the saucepan of simmering water, ensuring that the water level is comfortably lower than the basin's rim. Steam the pudding for 1 hour, topping up the water when necessary.

3 About 5 minutes before the end of the cooking time, heat the ingredients for the rum syrup in a small saucepan over low heat, stirring, until smooth and melted. Remove the pudding from the heat, discard the foil, and run a knife around the edge to loosen the pudding. Turn out onto a serving dish, pour over the syrup, and decorate with blueberries. Serve immediately.

exotic fruit chocolate crêpes

ingredients

SERVES 4

100 g/3½ oz plain flour
2 tbsp cocoa powder
pinch of salt
1 egg, beaten
300 ml/10 fl oz milk
oil, for frying
icing sugar, for dusting

filling

100 g/3½ oz thick plain yogurt
250 g/9 oz mascarpone cheese
icing sugar (optional)
1 mango, peeled and diced
225 g/8 oz strawberries, hulled and quartered
2 passion fruit

method

1 To make the filling, place the yogurt and mascarpone cheese in a bowl and sweeten with icing sugar, if you like. Place the mango and strawberries in a bowl and mix together. Cut the passion fruit in half, scoop out the pulp and seeds, and add to the mango and strawberries. Stir together, then set aside.

2 To make the crêpes, sift the flour, cocoa powder and salt into a bowl and make a well in the centre. Add the egg and whisk with a balloon whisk. Gradually beat in the milk, drawing in the flour from the sides, to make a smooth batter. Cover and set aside for 20 minutes. Heat a small amount of oil in an 18-cm/7-inch crêpe pan or frying pan. Pour in just enough batter to thinly coat the bottom of the pan. Cook over medium-high heat for 1 minute, then turn and cook the other side for 30–60 seconds, or until cooked through.

3 Transfer the crêpe to a plate and keep hot. Repeat with the remaining batter, stacking the cooked crêpes on top of each other with waxed paper in between. Keep warm in the oven while cooking the remainder. Divide the filling between the crêpes, then roll up and dust with icing sugar to serve.

chocolate ginger puddings

ingredients

SERVES 4

100 g/3½ oz soft margarine, plus extra for greasing
100 g/3½ oz self-raising flour, sifted
100 g/3½ oz caster sugar
2 eggs
25 g/1 oz cocoa powder, sifted
25 g/1 oz plain chocolate
50 g/1¾ oz stem ginger
icing sugar, for dusting

chocolate custard

2 egg yolks
1 tbsp caster sugar
1 tbsp cornflour
300 g/10 fl oz milk
100 g/3½ oz plain chocolate, broken into pieces

method

1 Lightly grease 4 small individual ovenproof bowls. Place the margarine, flour, sugar, eggs and cocoa in a mixing bowl and beat until well combined and smooth. Chop the chocolate and stem ginger and stir into the mixture, ensuring they are well combined.

2 Divide the cake mixture between the prepared bowls and smooth the tops. Cover the bowls with disks of baking parchment and cover with a pleated sheet of foil. Steam the mini chocolate gingers for 45 minutes until the sponges are cooked and springy to the touch.

3 Meanwhile, make the custard. Beat the egg yolks, sugar and cornflour together to form a smooth paste. Heat the milk until boiling and pour over the egg mixture. Return to the saucepan and cook over very low heat, stirring until thick. Remove from the heat and beat in the chocolate. Stir until the chocolate melts.

4 Lift the chocolate gingers from the steamer, run a knife around the edge of the bowls and carefully turn out onto serving plates. Dust each chocolate ginger with sugar and drizzle chocolate custard over the top. Serve the remaining chocolate custard separately.

sticky chocolate puddings

ingredients

SERVES 6

125 g/4$\frac{1}{2}$ oz butter, softened, plus extra for greasing
150 g/5$\frac{1}{2}$ oz brown sugar
3 eggs, beaten
pinch of salt
25 g/1 oz cocoa powder
125 g/4$\frac{1}{2}$ oz self-raising flour
25 g/1 oz plain chocolate, finely chopped
75 g/2$\frac{3}{4}$ oz white chocolate, finely chopped

sauce

150 ml/5 fl oz double cream
75 g/2$\frac{3}{4}$ oz brown sugar
2 tbsp butter

method

1 Lightly grease 6 individual 175-ml/6-fl oz individual dessert moulds.

2 Cream the butter and sugar together in a bowl until pale and fluffy. Beat in the eggs a little at a time, beating well after each addition. Sift the salt, cocoa and flour into the creamed mixture and fold in. Stir in the chopped chocolate until evenly combined throughout.

3 Divide the mixture between the prepared moulds. Lightly grease 6 squares of foil and use them to cover the tops of the moulds, pressing around the edges to seal. Place the moulds in a roasting pan and pour in boiling water to come halfway up the sides of the moulds. Bake in a preheated oven, 180°C/350°F, for 50 minutes or until a skewer inserted into the centre of the sponges comes out clean. Remove the moulds from the roasting pan and set aside.

4 To make the sauce, put the cream, sugar and butter into a saucepan and bring to the boil over gentle heat. Simmer gently until the sugar has completely dissolved.

5 To serve, run a knife around the edge of each sponge, then turn out onto serving plates. Serve immediately with the jug of sauce for pouring over.

individual chocolate puddings

ingredients

SERVES 4

puddings

100 g/3½ oz caster sugar
3 eggs
75 g/2¾ oz plain flour
50 g/1¾ oz cocoa powder
100 g/3½ oz unsalted butter, melted, plus extra for greasing
100 g/3½ oz plain chocolate, melted

chocolate sauce

2 tbsp unsalted butter
100 g/3½ oz plain chocolate
5 tbsp water
1 tbsp caster sugar
1 tbsp coffee-flavoured liqueur, such as Kahlua
coffee beans, to decorate

method

1 To make the puddings, put the sugar and eggs into a heatproof bowl and place over a saucepan of simmering water. Whisk for about 10 minutes until frothy. Remove the bowl from the heat and fold in the flour and cocoa. Fold in the butter, then the chocolate. Mix well. Grease 4 small heatproof bowls with butter. Spoon the mixture into the bowls and cover with waxed paper. Top with foil and secure with string. Place in a large saucepan filled with enough simmering water to reach halfway up the sides of the bowls. Steam for about 40 minutes, or until cooked through.

2 About 2–3 minutes before the end of the cooking time, make the sauce. Put the butter, chocolate, water and sugar into a small saucepan and warm over low heat, stirring constantly, until melted. Stir in the liqueur.

3 Remove the puddings from the heat, turn out into serving dishes, and pour over the sauce. Decorate with coffee beans and serve.

cappuccino soufflé puddings

ingredients

SERVES 6

butter, for greasing
2 tbsp golden caster sugar, plus extra for coating
6 tbsp whipping cream
2 tsp instant espresso coffee granules
2 tbsp Kahlua
3 large eggs, separated, plus 1 extra egg white
150 g/5½ oz plain chocolate, melted and cooled
cocoa powder, for dusting
chocolate-coated biscuits, to serve

method

1 Lightly grease the sides of 6 x 175-ml/6-fl oz ramekins with butter and coat with caster sugar. Place the ramekins on a baking sheet.

2 Place the cream in a small, heavy-based saucepan and heat gently. Stir in the coffee until it has dissolved, then stir in the Kahlua. Divide the coffee mixture between the prepared ramekins.

3 Place the egg whites in a clean, greasefree bowl and whisk until soft peaks form, then gradually whisk in the sugar until stiff but not dry. Stir the egg yolks and melted chocolate together in a separate bowl, then stir in a little of the whisked egg whites. Gradually fold in the remaining egg whites.

4 Divide the mixture between the dishes. Bake in a preheated oven, 190°C/375°F, for 15 minutes, or until just set. Dust with cocoa powder and serve immediately with chocolate-coated biscuits.

chocolate zabaglione

ingredients

SERVES 4

4 egg yolks

4 tbsp caster sugar

50 g/1¾ oz plain chocolate

125 ml/4 fl oz Marsala wine

cocoa powder, for dusting

amaretti biscuits, to serve

method

1 Place the egg yolks and caster sugar in a large glass bowl and, using an electric whisk, whisk together until the mixture is very pale.

2 Grate the chocolate finely and, using a spatula, fold into the egg mixture. Fold the Marsala wine into the chocolate mixture.

3 Place the bowl over a saucepan of gently simmering water and set the electric whisk on the lowest speed or swap to a balloon whisk. Cook gently, whisking constantly, until the mixture thickens. Do not overcook or the mixture will curdle.

4 Spoon the hot mixture into 4 warmed glass dishes or coffee cups and dust with cocoa. Serve as soon as possible, while it is warm, light and fluffy, with amaretti biscuits.

chocolate fondue

ingredients

SERVES 6

1 pineapple
1 mango
12 physalis
250 g/9 oz fresh strawberries
250 g/9 oz deseeded green grapes

fondue

250 g/9 oz plain chocolate, broken into pieces
150 ml/5 fl oz double cream
2 tbsp brandy

method

1 Using a sharp knife, peel and core the pineapple, then cut the flesh into cubes. Peel the mango and cut the flesh into cubes. Peel back the papery outer skin of the physalis and twist at the top to make a 'handle'. Arrange the fruit on 6 serving plates and chill in the refrigerator.

2 To make the fondue, place the chocolate and cream in a fondue pot. Heat gently, stirring constantly, until the chocolate has melted. Stir in the brandy until thoroughly blended and the chocolate mixture is smooth.

3 Place the fondue pot over the burner to keep warm. To serve, allow each guest to dip the fruit into the sauce, using fondue forks or bamboo skewers.

chilled & iced desserts

Chilled and iced chocolate desserts have a wow factor that is hard to beat. Not suprisingly, most of them involve a generous quantity of cream as well as chocolate, making them even more heavenly! If you love the fluffy texture of mousse, aim for the Chocolate Terrine – there are three layers of mousse in milk, white and plain chocolate – and if cheesecake is your passion, there's a great choice in this chapter.

The chapter begins with some gorgeous ice cream recipes. Home-made ice cream is very easy to make, especially if you have an ice cream maker, and once you have made your own you will never want to buy commercial ice cream again.

If you do not have an ice cream maker and don't want to invest in one, you can still make perfect ice cream. Before you begin, set the freezer to its lowest temperature. Pour the prepared ice-cream mixture into a freezerproof container, uncovered, and freeze for 1–2 hours. When it starts to set around the edges, remove it from the freezer, turn it out into a bowl and stir it with a fork or beat in an electric mixer until smooth. Add any extra ingredients at this point. Return to the freezer and freeze for a further 2–3 hours, or until firm. Cover the container with a lid for storing. Transfer the ice cream to the refrigerator about 30 minutes before serving.

chocolate praline ice cream

ingredients

SERVES 4–6

85 g/3 oz plain chocolate, broken into pieces
300 ml/10 fl oz whole milk
275 g/10 oz caster sugar
3 egg yolks
300 ml/10 fl oz whipping cream

praline

100 g/3½ oz granulated sugar
2 tbsp water
55 g/2 oz blanched almonds
vegetable oil, for oiling

method

1 To prepare the praline, put the sugar, water and nuts in a large heavy-based saucepan and heat gently, stirring, to dissolve the sugar. Allow the mixture to bubble gently, without stirring, for 6–10 minutes, until lightly golden brown, then immediately pour it onto an oiled baking sheet and spread it out evenly. Cool for 1 hour, or until cold and hardened, then place it in a plastic bag and crush with a hammer.

2 To make the ice cream, put the chocolate and milk in a saucepan and heat gently, stirring, until the chocolate has melted and the mixture is smooth. Remove from the heat.

3 Whisk the sugar and egg yolks together in a large bowl until pale and the mixture leaves a trail when the whisk is lifted. Slowly add the milk mixture, stirring constantly with a wooden spoon. Strain the mixture into the rinsed-out pan and cook over low heat for 10–15 minutes, stirring all the time, until the mixture thickens enough to coat the back of the spoon. Do not let the mixture boil or it will curdle.

4 Remove the custard from the heat and let it cool for at least 1 hour, stirring from time to time to prevent a skin forming. Whip the cream until it holds its shape, then fold in the cold custard and churn the mixture in an ice cream maker. Just before the ice cream freezes, add the praline and churn to mix.

marbled chocolate & orange ice cream

ingredients

SERVES 6

1 tsp cornflour
1 tsp vanilla essence
3 egg yolks
300 ml/10 fl oz milk
175 g/6 oz white chocolate, chopped into small pieces
450 ml/16 fl oz double cream
115 g/4 oz orange-flavoured plain chocolate, broken into pieces
grated orange rind, to decorate
orange segments, to serve

method

1 Beat the cornflour, vanilla essence and egg yolks in a heatproof bowl until well blended. Pour the milk into a large, heavy-based saucepan and bring to the boil over low heat. Pour over the egg yolk mixture, stirring constantly.

2 Strain the mixture back into the pan and heat gently, stirring constantly, until thickened. Remove from the heat, add the white chocolate pieces and stir until melted. Stir in the cream. Set aside 150 ml/6 fl oz of the mixture and pour the remainder into a large freezerproof container. Cover and freeze for 2 hours, or until starting to set. Melt the orange-flavoured chocolate, stir into the reserved mixture and set aside.

3 Remove the partially frozen ice cream from the freezer and beat with a fork. Place spoonfuls of the orange chocolate mixture over the ice cream and swirl with a knife to give a marbled effect. Freeze for 8 hours, or overnight, until firm. Transfer to the refrigerator 30 minutes before serving. Scoop into individual glasses, decorate with orange rind and serve with a few orange segments.

rich chocolate ice cream

ingredients

SERVES 6

ice cream

1 egg

3 egg yolks

85 g/3 oz caster sugar

300 ml/10 fl oz whole milk

250 g/9 oz plain chocolate

250 g/10 fl oz double cream

trellis cups

100 g/3½ oz plain chocolate

method

1 Beat the egg, egg yolks and caster sugar together in a mixing bowl until well combined. Heat the milk until it is almost boiling, then gradually pour it onto the eggs, whisking. Place the bowl over a saucepan of gently simmering water and cook, stirring constantly, until the custard mixture thickens sufficiently to thinly coat the back of a wooden spoon.

2 Break the chocolate into small pieces and add to the hot custard. Stir until the chocolate has melted. Cover with a sheet of dampened baking parchment and let it cool.

3 Whip the cream until just holding its shape, then fold into the cooled chocolate custard. Transfer to a freezerproof container and freeze for 1–2 hours until the mixture is frozen 2.5 cm/1 inch from the sides. Scrape the ice cream into a chilled bowl and beat again until smooth. Re-freeze until firm.

4 To make the trellis cups, invert a muffin pan and cover 6 alternate mounds with clingfilm. Melt the chocolate, place it in a paper pastry bag, and snip off the end.

5 Pipe a circle around the bottom of the mound, then pipe chocolate back and forth over it to form a double-thickness trellis. Pipe around the bottom again. Chill until set, then lift from the pan and remove the clingfilm. Serve the ice cream in the trellis cups.

chocolate chip & fudge banana ice cream

ingredients

SERVES 6

4 ripe bananas
juice of 1/2 lemon
200 g/7 oz golden caster sugar
500 ml/18 fl oz whipping cream
100 g/3 1/2 oz plain chocolate chips
100 g/3 1/2 oz fudge, cut into small pieces, plus extra to decorate

method

1 Peel the bananas and chop them coarsely, then place in a food processor with the lemon juice and sugar. Process until well chopped, then pour in the cream and process again until well blended.

2 Freeze in an ice cream maker, following the manufacturer's instructions, adding the chocolate chips and fudge just before the ice cream is ready.

3 Transfer the ice cream to the refrigerator 15 minutes before serving. Scoop into small bowls to serve and decorate with extra fudge pieces.

coconut & white chocolate ice cream

ingredients

SERVES 6

2 eggs
2 egg yolks
115 g/4 oz golden caster sugar
300 ml/10 fl oz single cream
115 g/4 oz white chocolate, chopped
115 g/4 oz creamed coconut, chopped
300 ml/10 fl oz double cream
3 tbsp coconut rum
tropical fruit, such as mango, pineapple or passion fruit, to serve

method

1 Place the whole eggs, egg yolks and sugar in a heatproof bowl and beat together until well blended. Place the single cream, chocolate and coconut in a saucepan and heat gently until the chocolate has melted, then continue to heat, stirring constantly, until almost boiling. Pour onto the egg mixture, stirring vigorously, then set the bowl over a saucepan of gently simmering water, making sure that the base of the bowl does not touch the water.

2 Heat the mixture, stirring constantly, until it lightly coats the back of the spoon. Strain into a clean, heatproof bowl and allow it to cool. Place the double cream and rum in a separate bowl and whip until slightly thickened, then fold into the cooled chocolate mixture.

3 Freeze in an ice cream maker, following the manufacturer's instructions. Transfer the ice cream to the refrigerator for 30 minutes before serving. Scoop into small serving bowls and serve with tropical fruit.

white chocolate ice cream

ingredients

SERVES 6

ice cream

1 egg, plus 1 extra egg yolk
3 tbsp caster sugar
150 g/5½ oz white chocolate
300 ml/10 fl oz milk
150 ml/5 fl oz double cream

biscuit cups

1 egg white
4 tbsp caster sugar
2 tbsp plain flour, sifted
2 tbsp cocoa powder, sifted
2 tbsp butter, melted

plain chocolate, melted, to serve

method

1 Line 2 baking sheets with baking parchment. To make the ice cream, beat the egg, egg yolk and sugar together. Break the chocolate into pieces, place in a bowl with 3 tablespoons of milk, and melt over a saucepan of hot water. Heat the milk until almost boiling and pour onto the eggs, whisking. Place over a saucepan of simmering water and stir until the mixture thickens. Whisk in the chocolate. Cover with dampened baking parchment and let cool.

2 Whip the cream and fold into the custard. Transfer to a freezerproof container and freeze the mixture for 1–2 hours. Scrape into a bowl and beat until smooth. Re-freeze until firm.

3 To make the biscuit cups, beat the egg white and sugar. Beat in the flour and cocoa powder, then the butter. Place 1 tablespoon on 1 baking sheet and spread out into a 12.5-cm/5-inch circle. Bake in a preheated oven, 200°C/400°F, for 4–5 minutes. Remove and mould over an upturned cup. Let it set, then cool. Repeat to make 6 biscuit cups. Serve the ice cream in the cups, drizzled with melted chocolate.

sicilian cassata

ingredients

SERVES 8

150 g/5½ oz self-raising flour
2 tbsp cocoa powder
1 tsp baking powder
175 g/6 oz butter, softened, plus extra for greasing
175 g/6 oz golden caster sugar
3 eggs
icing sugar, for dusting
chocolate curls, to decorate

filling

450 g/1 lb ricotta cheese
100 g/3½ oz plain chocolate, grated
115 g/4 oz golden caster sugar
3 tbsp Marsala wine
55 g/2 oz chopped candied peel
2 tbsp almonds, chopped

method

1 Sift the flour, cocoa powder and baking powder into a large bowl. Add the butter, sugar and eggs and beat together thoroughly until smooth and creamy. Pour the cake batter into a greased and base-lined 18-cm/7-inch round cake tin and bake in a preheated oven, 375°F/ 190°C, for 30–40 minutes, or until well risen and firm to the touch. Let stand in the tin for 5 minutes, then turn out onto a wire rack to cool completely.

2 Wash and dry the cake tin and grease and line it again. To make the filling, rub the ricotta through a sieve into a bowl. Add the grated chocolate, sugar and Marsala wine and beat together until the mixture is light and fluffy. Stir in the candied peel and almonds.

3 Cut the thin crust off the top of the cake and discard. Cut the cake horizontally into 3 layers. Place the first slice in the prepared tin and cover with half the ricotta mixture. Repeat the layers, finishing with a cake layer. Press down lightly, cover with a plate and a weight, and chill in the refrigerator for 8 hours, or overnight. To serve, turn the cake out onto a serving plate. Dust with icing sugar and decorate with chocolate curls.

zucotto

ingredients

SERVES 6

- 115 g/4 oz soft margarine, plus extra for greasing
- 100 g/3½ oz self-raising flour
- 2 tbsp cocoa powder
- ½ tsp baking powder
- 115 g/4 oz golden caster sugar
- 2 eggs, beaten
- 3 tbsp brandy
- 2 tbsp Kirsch

filling

- 300 ml/10 fl oz double cream
- 25 g/1 oz icing sugar, sifted
- 55 g/2 oz toasted almonds, chopped
- 225 g/8 oz black cherries, pitted
- 55 g/2 oz plain chocolate, finely chopped

to decorate

- 1 tbsp cocoa powder
- 1 tbsp icing sugar
- fresh cherries

method

1 Grease a 30 x 23-cm/12 x 9-inch Swiss roll tin and line it with baking parchment. Sift the flour, cocoa and baking powder into a bowl. Add the sugar, margarine and eggs. Beat together until well mixed, then spoon into the prepared tin. Bake in a preheated oven, 375°F/190°C, for 15–20 minutes, or until well risen and firm to the touch. Let it stand in the tin for 5 minutes, then turn out onto a wire rack to cool.

2 Using the rim of a 1.2-litre/2½ pint ovenproof bowl as a guide, cut a circle from the cake and set aside. Line the bowl with clingfilm. Use the remaining cake, cutting it as necessary, to line the bowl. Place the brandy and Kirsch in a small bowl and mix together. Sprinkle over the cake, including the reserved circle.

3 To make the filling, pour the cream into a separate bowl and add the icing sugar. Whip until thick, then fold in the almonds, cherries and chocolate. Fill the sponge mould with the cream mixture and press the cake circle on top. Cover with a plate and a weight, and chill in the refrigerator for 6–8 hours, or overnight. When ready to serve, turn the zucotto out onto a serving plate. Decorate with cocoa and icing sugar, sifted over in alternating segments, and a few cherries.

iced white chocolate terrine

ingredients

SERVES 8

2 tbsp granulated sugar
5 tbsp water
300 g/10½ oz white chocolate
3 eggs, separated
300 ml/10 fl oz double cream
strawberry coulis and fresh strawberries, to serve

method

1 Line a 450-g/1-lb loaf tin with foil, pressing out as many creases as you can.

2 Place the granulated sugar and water in a heavy-based saucepan and heat gently, stirring until the sugar has dissolved. Bring to the boil, then boil for 1–2 minutes until syrupy. Remove the pan from the heat.

3 Break the white chocolate into small pieces and stir it into the syrup, continuing to stir until the chocolate has melted and combined with the syrup. Set aside to cool slightly. Beat the egg yolks into the chocolate mixture, then cool completely.

4 Lightly whip the cream until just holding its shape, and fold it into the chocolate mixture. Whisk the egg whites in a clean bowl until they are standing in soft peaks. Fold the whites into the chocolate mixture. Pour into the prepared loaf tin and freeze overnight.

5 To serve, remove the terrine from the freezer about 10–15 minutes before serving and remove the foil. Turn out of the tin and cut into slices to serve.

champagne mousse

ingredients

SERVES 4

sponge

4 eggs

100 g/3½ oz caster sugar

75 g/2¾ oz self-raising flour

2 tbsp cocoa powder

2 tbsp butter, melted

mousse

1 envelope powdered gelatine

3 tbsp water

300 ml/10 fl oz champagne

300 ml/10 fl oz double cream

2 egg whites

6 tbsp caster sugar

to decorate

50 g/2 oz plain chocolate-flavoured cake covering, melted

method

1 Line a 38 x 25-cm/15 x 10-inch Swiss roll tin with greased baking parchment. Place the eggs and sugar in a bowl and beat, using an electric mixer, until the mixture is very thick and the whisk leaves a trail when lifted. Sieve the flour and cocoa together and fold into the egg mixture. Fold in the butter. Pour into the tin and bake in a preheated oven, 200°C/400°F, for 8 minutes or until springy to the touch. Cool in the tin for 5 minutes, then turn out onto a wire rack until cold. Meanwhile, line 4 x 10-cm/4-inch baking rings with baking parchment. Line the sides with 2.5-cm/1-inch strips of cake and the bottom with circles.

2 For the mousse, sprinkle the gelatine over the water and let it go spongy. Place the bowl over a saucepan of hot water and stir until the gelatine has dissolved. Stir in the champagne.

3 Whip the cream until just holding its shape. Fold in the champagne mixture. Stand in a cool place until on the point of setting, stirring. Whisk the egg whites until standing in soft peaks, add the sugar and whisk until glossy. Carefully fold the egg whites into the setting mixture. Spoon into the sponge cases, allowing the mixture to go above the sponge. Chill for 2 hours. Pipe the cake covering in squiggles on a piece of parchment, let them set, then use to decorate the mousses.

white chocolate mousse

ingredients

SERVES 6

250 g/9 oz white chocolate, broken into pieces
100 ml/3½ fl oz milk
300 ml/10 fl oz double cream
1 tsp rose water
2 egg whites
115 g/4 oz plain chocolate, broken into pieces
candied rose petals, to decorate

method

1 Place the white chocolate and milk in a saucepan and heat gently until the chocolate has melted, then stir. Transfer to a large bowl and leave to cool.

2 Place the cream and rose water in a separate bowl and whip until soft peaks form. Whisk the egg whites in a separate spotlessly clean, greasefree bowl until stiff but not dry. Gently fold the whipped cream into the white chocolate, then fold in the egg whites. Spoon the mixture into 6 small dishes or glasses, cover with clingfilm and chill for 8 hours, or overnight, to set.

3 Melt the plain chocolate and let it cool, then pour evenly over the mousses. Stand until the chocolate has hardened, then decorate with rose petals and serve.

white chocolate moulds

ingredients

SERVES 6

- 125 g/4½ oz white chocolate, broken into pieces
- 250 ml/9 fl oz double cream
- 3 tbsp crème fraîche
- 2 eggs, separated
- 3 tbsp water
- 1½ tsp powdered gelatine
- oil, for brushing
- 140 g/5 oz sliced strawberries
- 140 g/5 oz raspberries
- 140 g/5 oz blackcurrants
- 5 tbsp caster sugar
- 125 ml/4 fl oz crème de framboise
- 12 blackcurrant leaves, if available

method

1 Put the chocolate in a heatproof bowl set over a saucepan of barely simmering water. Stir over a low heat until melted and smooth. Remove from the heat and set aside.

2 Pour the cream into a saucepan and bring to just below boiling point over low heat. Remove from the heat, then stir the cream and crème fraîche into the chocolate and allow to cool slightly. Beat in the egg yolks, one at a time.

3 Pour the water into the bowl and sprinkle over the gelatine. Leave for 2–3 minutes to soften, then set over a saucepan of barely simmering water until dissolved. Stir into the chocolate mixture and set aside until nearly set.

4 Brush the insides of 6 timbales or ramekins with oil and line the bases with parchment paper. Whisk the egg whites until soft peaks form, then fold them into the chocolate mixture. Divide the mixture between the moulds and smooth the surface. Cover with clingfilm and chill for 2 hours, until set.

5 Put the strawberries, raspberries and blackcurrants in a bowl. Sprinkle with the caster sugar, then gently stir in the liqueur. Cover with clingfilm and chill for 2 hours.

6 To serve, run a round-bladed knife around the moulds and turn out onto individual plates. Divide the fruit between the plates and serve decorated with blackcurrant leaves.

chocolate rum pots

ingredients

SERVES 6

225 g/8 oz plain chocolate
4 eggs, separated
6 tbsp caster sugar
4 tbsp dark rum
4 tbsp double cream

to decorate

a little whipped cream (optional)
marbled chocolate shapes

method

1 Melt the plain chocolate and let it cool slightly. Whisk the egg yolks with the caster sugar in a bowl until very pale and fluffy. Drizzle the chocolate into the egg yolk and sugar mixture and fold in together with the dark rum and the double cream.

2 Whisk the egg whites in a clean bowl until standing in soft peaks. Fold the egg whites into the chocolate mixture in 2 batches. Divide the mixture between 6 individual dishes, and chill for at least 2 hours before serving.

3 To serve, decorate with a little whipped cream if liked and a marbled chocolate shape.

chocolate & orange pots

ingredients

SERVES 6

200 g/7 oz plain chocolate, broken into pieces
grated rind of 1 orange
300 ml/10 fl oz double cream
140 g/5 oz golden caster sugar
3 tbsp Cointreau
3 large egg whites
fine strips of orange rind, to decorate
crisp biscuits, to serve

method

1 Melt the chocolate and stir in the orange rind. Place the cream in a bowl with 100 g/ 3½ oz of the sugar and the Cointreau and whip until thick.

2 Place the egg whites in a spotlessly clean, greasefree bowl and whisk until soft peaks form, then gradually whisk in the remaining sugar until stiff but not dry. Fold the melted chocolate into the cream, then beat in a spoonful of the whisked egg whites. Gently fold in the remaining egg whites until thoroughly mixed.

3 Spoon the mixture into 8 small ramekin dishes or demi-tasse coffee cups. Cover and chill in the refrigerator for 1 hour, then decorate with a few strips of orange rind before serving with crisp biscuits.

chocolate & strawberry brûlées

ingredients

SERVES 6

250 g/9 oz fresh strawberries, washed and hulled
2 tbsp fruit liqueur, such as Kirsch or crème de cassis
450 ml/16 fl oz double cream
115 g/4 oz plain chocolate, melted and cooled
115 g/4 oz raw brown sugar

to decorate

fresh strawberries
fresh mint leaves

method

1 Cut the strawberries into halves or quarters, depending on their size, and divide between 6 ramekins. Sprinkle with the fruit liqueur.

2 Pour the cream into a bowl and whip until it is just holding its shape. Add the cooled chocolate and continue whipping until the cream is thick. Spread over the strawberries. Cover and place in the freezer for 2 hours, or until the cream is frozen.

3 Preheat the grill to high. Sprinkle the sugar thickly over the cream, then place under the hot grill and cook until the sugar has melted and caramelized. Let the brûlées stand for 30 minutes, or until the fruit and cream have thawed. Serve decorated with a few fresh strawberries and mint leaves.

coffee panna cotta with chocolate sauce

ingredients

SERVES 6

oil, for brushing
600 ml/1 pint double cream
1 vanilla pod
55 g/2 oz golden caster sugar
2 tsp instant espresso coffee granules, dissolved in 4 tbsp water
2 tsp powdered gelatine
chocolate-covered coffee beans, to serve

sauce

150 ml/5 fl oz single cream
55 g/2 oz plain chocolate, melted

method

1 Lightly brush 6 x 5-fl oz/150-ml moulds with oil. Place the cream in a saucepan. Split the vanilla pod and scrape the black seeds into the cream. Add the vanilla pod and the sugar, then heat gently until almost boiling. Sieve the cream into a heatproof bowl and reserve. Place the coffee in a small heatproof bowl, sprinkle on the gelatine and leave for 5 minutes, or until spongy. Set the bowl over a saucepan of gently simmering water until the gelatine has dissolved.

2 Stir a little of the reserved cream into the gelatin mixture, then stir the gelatine mixture into the remainder of the cream. Divide the mixture between the prepared moulds and cool, then chill in the refrigerator for 8 hours, or overnight.

3 To make the sauce, place one quarter of the cream in a bowl and stir in the melted chocolate. Gradually stir in the remaining cream, reserving 1 tablespoon. To serve the panna cotta, dip the bases of the moulds briefly into hot water and turn out onto 6 dessert plates. Pour the chocolate cream around. Dot drops of the reserved cream onto the sauce and feather it with a skewer. Decorate with chocolate-covered coffee beans and serve.

chocolate coeurs à la crème

ingredients

SERVES 8

225 g/8 oz ricotta cheese
55 g/2 oz icing sugar, sifted
300 ml/10 fl oz double cream
1 tsp vanilla essence
55 g/2 oz plain chocolate, grated
2 egg whites

coulis

225 g/8 oz fresh raspberries
icing sugar, to taste

to decorate

fresh strawberries, halved
fresh raspberries

method

1 Line 8 individual moulds with cheesecloth. Press the ricotta cheese through a sieve into a bowl. Add the icing sugar, cream and vanilla essence and beat together thoroughly. Stir in the grated chocolate. Place the egg whites in a separate clean bowl and whisk until stiff but not dry. Gently fold into the cheese mixture.

2 Spoon the mixture into the prepared moulds. Stand the moulds on a tray or dish and let them drain in the refrigerator for 8 hours, or overnight – the cheesecloth will absorb most of the liquid.

3 To make the raspberry coulis, place the raspberries in a food processor and process to a purée. Press the purée through a sieve into a bowl and add icing sugar, to taste. To serve, turn each dessert out onto a serving plate and pour the raspberry coulis round. Decorate with strawberries and raspberries, then serve.

chocolate marquise

ingredients

SERVES 6

200 g/7 oz plain chocolate
100 g/3½ oz butter
3 egg yolks
75 g/2¾ oz caster sugar
1 tsp chocolate extract or
  1 tbsp chocolate-flavoured
  liqueur
300 ml/10 fl oz double cream

to serve

chocolate-dipped fruits
crème fraîche
cocoa powder, for dusting

method

1 Break the chocolate into pieces. Place the chocolate and butter in a bowl set over a saucepan of gently simmering water and stir until melted and well combined. Remove the pan from the heat and let the chocolate cool.

2 Place the egg yolks in a mixing bowl with the sugar and whisk until pale and fluffy. Using an electric mixer running on low speed, slowly whisk in the cool chocolate mixture. Stir in the chocolate extract or chocolate-flavoured liqueur.

3 Whip the cream until just holding its shape. Fold into the chocolate mixture. Spoon into 6 small custard pots or individual metal moulds. Chill the desserts for at least 2 hours.

4 To serve, turn out the desserts onto individual serving dishes. If you have difficulty turning them out, first dip the pots or moulds into a bowl of warm water for a few seconds. Serve with chocolate-dipped fruit and crème fraîche and dust with cocoa.

marble cheesecake

ingredients

SERVES 10

base

225 g/8 oz toasted oat cereal
50 g/$1^{3}/_{4}$ oz toasted hazelnuts, chopped
4 tbsp butter
25 g/1 oz plain chocolate

filling

350 g/12 oz full-fat soft cheese
100 g/$3^{1}/_{2}$ oz caster sugar
200 ml/7 fl oz thick yogurt
300 ml/10 fl oz double cream
1 envelope powdered gelatine
3 tbsp water
175 g/6 oz plain chocolate, melted
175 g/6 oz white chocolate, melted

method

1 Place the toasted oat cereal in a plastic bag and crush it roughly with a rolling pin. Pour the crushed cereal into a mixing bowl and stir in the toasted chopped hazelnuts.

2 Melt the butter and chocolate together over low heat and stir into the cereal mixture, stirring until well coated.

3 Using the bottom of a glass, press the mixture into the bottom and up the sides of a 20-cm/8-inch springform cake tin.

4 Beat the cheese and sugar together with a wooden spoon until smooth. Beat in the yogurt. Whip the cream until just holding its shape and fold into the mixture. Sprinkle the gelatine over the water in a heatproof bowl and let it go spongy. Place over a saucepan of hot water and stir until dissolved. Stir into the mixture.

5 Divide the mixture in half and beat the plain chocolate into one half and the white chocolate into the other half.

6 Place alternate spoonfuls of mixture on top of the cereal base. Swirl the filling together with the tip of a knife to give a marbled effect. Smooth the top with a spatula. Chill the cheesecake for at least 2 hours, until set, before serving.

irish cream cheesecake

ingredients

SERVES 12

oil, for brushing
175 g/6 oz chocolate chip cookies
55 g/2 oz butter

filling

225 g/8 oz plain chocolate
225 g/8 oz milk chocolate
55 g/2 oz golden caster sugar
350 g/12 oz cream cheese
425 ml/15 fl oz double cream, whipped
3 tbsp Irish cream liqueur

to serve

crème fraîche or sour cream
fresh fruit

method

1 Line the base of a 20-cm/8-inch springform tin with foil and brush the sides with oil. Place the cookies in a polythene bag and crush with a rolling pin. Place the butter in a saucepan and heat gently until just melted, then stir in the crushed cookies. Press the mixture into the base of the tin and chill in the refrigerator for 1 hour.

2 To make the filling, melt the plain and milk chocolate together, stir to combine and leave to cool. Place the sugar and cream cheese in a large bowl and beat together until smooth, then fold in the whipped cream. Fold the mixture gently into the melted chocolate, then stir in the Irish cream liqueur.

3 Spoon the filling over the chilled biscuit base and smooth the surface. Cover and chill in the refrigerator for 2 hours, or until quite firm. Transfer to a serving plate and cut into small slices. Serve with a spoonful of crème fraîche and fresh fruit.

banana coconut cheesecake

ingredients

SERVES 10

225 g/8 oz chocolate chip cookies
4 tbsp butter
350 g/12 oz medium-fat soft cheese
75 g/2¾ oz caster sugar
50 g/1¾ oz fresh coconut, grated
2 tbsp coconut-flavoured liqueur
2 ripe bananas
125 g/4½ oz plain chocolate
1 envelope powdered gelatine
3 tbsp water
150 ml/5 fl oz double cream

to decorate

1 banana
lemon juice
a little melted chocolate

method

1 Place the cookies in a plastic bag and crush with a rolling pin. Pour into a mixing bowl. Melt the butter and stir into the cookie crumbs until well coated. Firmly press the cookie mixture into the bottom and up the sides of a 20-cm/8-inch springform cake tin.

2 Beat the soft cheese and caster sugar together until well combined, then beat in the grated coconut and coconut-flavoured liqueur. Mash the 2 bananas and beat them in. Melt the plain chocolate and beat into the mixture until well combined.

3 Sprinkle the gelatine over the water in a heatproof bowl and let it go spongy. Place over a saucepan of hot water and stir until dissolved. Stir into the chocolate mixture. Whip the cream until just holding its shape and stir into the chocolate mixture. Spoon the filling over the biscuit shell and chill for 2 hours, until set.

4 To serve, carefully transfer to a serving plate. Slice the banana, toss in the lemon juice and arrange around the edge of the cheesecake. Drizzle with melted chocolate and allow to set before serving.

chocolate terrine with orange cream

ingredients

SERVES 10–12

6 tbsp water
3 tsp powdered gelatine
115 g/4 oz each of milk, white and plain chocolate, broken into pieces
450 ml/16 fl oz whipping cream
6 eggs, separated
75 g/2¾ oz caster sugar

orange cream

2 tbsp caster sugar
1 tbsp cornflour
2 egg yolks
150 ml/5 fl oz milk
150 ml/5 fl oz double cream
grated rind of 1 orange
1 tbsp Cointreau

to decorate

150 ml/5 fl oz double cream, whipped
chocolate-covered coffee beans
orange zest

method

1 To make the milk chocolate mousse, place 2 tablespoons of the water in a heatproof bowl. Sprinkle on 1 teaspoon of gelatine and stand for 5 minutes. Set the bowl over a saucepan of simmering water until the gelatine has dissolved. Let it cool. Melt the milk chocolate and let it cool. Whip one-third of the cream until thick. Whisk 2 of the egg whites in a bowl until stiff but not dry. Whisk 2 of the egg yolks and one third of the sugar in a separate bowl until thick. Stir in the chocolate, gelatine and whipped cream. Fold in the whisked egg whites.

2 Pour into a 1.2-litre/2¾-pint loaf tin, lined with clingfilm. Cover and freeze for 20 minutes, or until set. Make the white chocolate mousse in the same way, pour over the milk chocolate mousse and freeze. Make the plain chocolate mousse and pour on top. Chill for 2 hours, until set.

3 To make the orange cream, stir the sugar, cornflour and egg yolks together until smooth. Heat the milk, cream and orange rind in a saucepan until almost boiling, then pour over the egg mixture, whisking. Strain back into the pan and heat until thick. Cover and cool, then stir in the Cointreau. Turn out the terrine and decorate with cream, coffee beans and orange zest.

chocolate & cherry tiramisù

ingredients

SERVES 4

- 7 fl oz/200 ml strong black coffee, cooled to room temperature
- 6 tbsp cherry brandy
- 16 trifle sponges
- 250 g/9 oz mascarpone
- 300 ml/10 fl oz double cream, lightly whipped
- 3 tbsp confectioner's sugar
- 275 g/9½ oz sweet cherries, halved and pitted
- 60 g/2¼ oz chocolate, curls or grated
- whole cherries, to decorate

method

1 Pour the cooled coffee into a jug and stir in the cherry brandy. Put half of the trifle sponges into the bottom of a serving dish, then pour over half of the coffee mixture.

2 Put the mascarpone into a separate bowl along with the cream and sugar, and mix well. Spread half of the mascarpone mixture over the coffee-soaked trifle sponges, then top with half of the cherries. Arrange the remaining trifle sponges on top. Pour over the remaining coffee mixture and top with the remaining cherries. Finish with a layer of mascarpone mixture. Scatter over the grated chocolate, cover with clingfilm and chill in the refrigerator for at least 2 hours.

3 Remove from the refrigerator, decorate with cherries, and serve.

chocolate trifle

ingredients

SERVES 4

280 g/10 oz ready-made chocolate loaf cake
3–4 tbsp seeded raspberry jam
4 tbsp amaretto liqueur
250 g/9 oz package frozen mixed red fruit, thawed

custard

6 egg yolks
55 g/2 oz golden caster sugar
1 tbsp cornflour
500 ml/18 fl oz milk
55 g/2 oz plain chocolate, melted

topping

225 ml/8 fl oz double cream
1 tbsp golden caster sugar
1/2 tsp vanilla essence

to decorate

ready-made chocolate truffles
fresh fruit, such as cherries and strawberries

method

1 Cut the cake into slices and make 'sandwiches' with the raspberry jam. Cut the sandwiches into cubes and place in a large serving bowl. Sprinkle with the amaretto liqueur. Spread the fruit over the cake.

2 To make the custard, place the egg yolks and sugar in a heatproof bowl and whisk until thick and pale, then stir in the cornflour. Place the milk in a saucepan and heat until almost boiling. Pour onto the egg yolk mixture, stirring. Return the mixture to the pan and bring just to the boil, stirring constantly, until it thickens. Remove from the heat and let cool slightly. Stir in the melted chocolate. Pour the custard over the cake and fruit. Let cool, then cover and chill in the refrigerator for 2 hours, or until set.

3 To make the topping, whip the cream until soft peaks form, then beat in the sugar and vanilla essence. Spoon over the trifle. Decorate with the truffles and fruit and chill until ready to serve.

cakes & tortes

This chapter starts with a Devil's Food Cake, a hint of wickedness that sets the tone for all the other recipes. There is no point in pretending that these delicious cakes and tortes are anything less than pure, unadulterated indulgence, although if you think a hint of fruit or vegetables might lend a slightly virtuous air, you could try the Date and Chocolate Cake or the Chocolate Passion Cake! Be warned, however – the grated carrots in the passion cake only serve to make it irresistibly moist, so you probably won't be able to resist a second slice.

There's a decidedly grown-up feel to most of the cakes in this selection, and indeed many of them would make a stylish dessert to end an elegant dinner party – the Mocha Layer Cake, perhaps, or the Chocolate Truffle Torte. Your guests will love you!

So that the young ones don't feel left out, though, there's a lovely Family Chocolate Cake, ideal for Sunday afternoon tea. There are some pretty little cupcakes, too, which would be perfect served at a children's party – with plenty of napkins at hand for mopping up, because they are delightfully messy to eat. In the middle of each Warm Molten-centred Cupcake is a square of pure chocolate, which spills out when you bite into it. Mmm!

devil's food cake

ingredients

SERVES 10–12

100 g/3½ oz plain chocolate
250 g/9 oz self-raising flour
1 tsp bicarbonate of soda
225 g/8 oz butter, plus extra for greasing
400 g/14 oz dark brown sugar
1 tsp vanilla essence
3 eggs
125 ml/4 fl oz buttermilk
225 ml/8 fl oz boiling water

frosting

300 g/10½ oz caster sugar
2 egg whites
1 tbsp lemon juice
3 tbsp orange juice
candied orange peel, to decorate

method

1 Melt the chocolate in a heatproof bowl over a saucepan of simmering water. Sift the flour and bicarbonate of soda together.

2 Place the butter and sugar in a large bowl and beat until pale and fluffy. Beat in the vanilla essence and the eggs, one at a time, beating well after each addition. Add a little flour if the mixture starts to curdle. Fold the melted chocolate into the mixture until well blended. Fold in the remaining flour, then stir in the buttermilk and the boiling water.

3 Divide the mixture between 2 lightly greased and base-lined 20-cm/8-inch shallow round cake tins and level the tops. Bake in a preheated oven, 190°C/375°F, for 30 minutes, or until springy to the touch. Cool in the pan for 5 minutes, then transfer to a wire rack and cool completely.

4 Place the frosting ingredients in a large bowl set over a pan of simmering water. Using an electric whisk, whisk until thick and forming soft peaks. Remove from the heat and whisk until the mixture is cool.

5 Sandwich the 2 cakes together with a little of the frosting, then spread the remainder over the sides and top of the cake. Decorate with candied orange peel.

mocha layer cake

ingredients

SERVES 8

200 g/7 oz self-raising flour
1/4 tsp baking powder
4 tbsp cocoa powder
100 g/3 1/2 oz caster sugar
2 eggs
2 tbsp golden syrup
150 ml/5 fl oz corn oil
150 ml/5 fl oz milk
butter for greasing

filling

1 tsp instant coffee
1 tbsp boiling water
300 ml/10 fl oz double cream
2 tbsp icing sugar

to decorate

50 g/1 3/4 oz plain chocolate, grated
chocolate caraque
icing sugar, for dusting

method

1 Sift the flour, baking powder and cocoa into a large bowl, then stir in the sugar. Make a well in the centre and stir in the eggs, syrup, corn oil and milk. Beat with a wooden spoon, gradually mixing in the dry ingredients to make a smooth batter. Divide the mixture between 3 lightly greased 18-cm/7-inch cake tins.

2 Bake in a preheated oven, 180°C/350°F, for 35–45 minutes, or until springy to the touch. Cool in the tins for 5 minutes, then turn out and cool completely on a wire rack.

3 To make the filling, dissolve the instant coffee in the boiling water and place in a large bowl with the cream and icing sugar. Whip until the cream is just holding its shape, then use half the cream to sandwich the 3 cakes together. Spread the remaining cream over the top and sides of the cake. Press the grated chocolate into the cream round the edge of the cake.

4 Transfer the cake to a serving plate. Lay the chocolate caraque over the top of the cake. Cut a few thin strips of baking parchment and place on top of the chocolate caraque. Dust lightly with icing sugar, then carefully remove the parchment. Serve.

chocolate ganache cake

ingredients

SERVES 10

175 g/6 oz butter
175 g/6 oz caster sugar
4 eggs, beaten lightly
200 g/7 oz self-raising flour
1 tbsp cocoa powder
50 g/1¾ oz plain chocolate, melted

ganache

450 ml/16 fl oz double cream
375 g/13 oz plain chocolate, broken into pieces
200 g/7 oz chocolate-flavoured cake covering, to finish

method

1 Beat the butter and sugar until light and fluffy. Gradually add the eggs, beating well. Sift the flour and cocoa together. Fold into the cake mixture. Fold in the melted chocolate.

2 Pour into a lightly greased and base-lined 20-cm/8-inch springform cake tin and smooth the top. Bake in a preheated oven, 180°C/350°F, for 40 minutes or until springy to the touch. Cool for 5 minutes in the tin, then turn out onto a wire rack to cool completely. Cut the cold cake into 2 layers.

3 To make the ganache, place the cream in a saucepan and bring to the boil, stirring. Add the chocolate and stir until melted and combined. Pour into a bowl and whisk for about 5 minutes or until fluffy and cool. Set aside one third of the ganache and use the rest to sandwich the cake together and spread smoothly and evenly over the top and sides of the cake.

4 Melt the cake covering and spread it over a large sheet of baking parchment. Cool until just set. Cut into strips a little wider than the height of the cake. Place the strips around the edge of the cake, overlapping them slightly.

5 Using a piping bag fitted with a fine tip, pipe the reserved ganache in tear drops or shells to cover the top of the cake. Chill for 1 hour in the refrigerator before serving.

chocolate cake with coffee syrup

ingredients

SERVES 12

- 225 g/8 oz plain chocolate, broken into pieces
- 115 g/4 oz unsalted butter, plus extra for greasing
- 1 tbsp strong black coffee
- 4 large eggs
- 2 egg yolks
- 115 g/4 oz golden caster sugar
- 55 g/2 oz plain flour
- 2 tsp ground cinnamon
- 50 g/1¾ oz ground almonds
- chocolate-covered coffee beans, to decorate

syrup

- 300 ml/10 fl oz strong black coffee
- 115 g/4 oz golden caster sugar
- 1 cinnamon stick

method

1 Place the chocolate, butter and coffee in a heatproof bowl and set over a pan of gently simmering water until melted. Stir to blend, then remove from the heat and cool slightly.

2 Place the whole eggs, egg yolks and sugar in a separate bowl and whisk together until thick and pale. Sift the flour and cinnamon over the egg mixture. Add the almonds and the chocolate mixture and fold in carefully. Spoon the batter into a greased and base-lined deep 20-cm/8-inch round cake tin. Bake in a preheated oven, 375°F/190°C, for 35 minutes, or until the tip of a knife inserted into the centre comes out clean. Cool slightly before turning out onto a serving plate.

3 Meanwhile, make the syrup. Place the coffee, sugar and cinnamon stick in a heavy-based saucepan and heat gently, stirring, until the sugar has dissolved. Increase the heat and boil for 5 minutes, or until reduced and thickened slightly. Keep warm. Pierce the surface of the cake with a cocktail stick, then drizzle over half the coffee syrup. Decorate with chocolate-covered coffee beans and serve, cut into wedges, with the remaining coffee syrup.

white truffle cake

ingredients

SERVES 12

2 eggs
4 tbsp caster sugar
55 g/2 oz plain flour
50 g/1¾ oz white chocolate, melted

truffle topping

300 ml/10 fl oz double cream
350 g/12 oz white chocolate, broken into pieces
250 g/9 oz mascarpone cheese

to decorate

plain, milk or white chocolate caraque
cocoa powder, for dusting

method

1 Whisk the eggs and caster sugar in a mixing bowl for 10 minutes or until the mixture is very light and foamy and the whisk leaves a trail that lasts a few seconds when lifted. Sift the flour and fold in with a metal spoon. Fold in the melted white chocolate. Pour into a greased and lined 20-cm/8-inch round springform cake tin and bake in a preheated oven, 180°C/350°F, for 25 minutes or until springy to the touch. Cool slightly in the tin, then transfer to a wire rack until completely cold. Return the cold cake to the tin.

2 To make the topping, place the cream in a pan and bring to the boil, stirring to prevent it sticking to the bottom of the pan. Cool slightly, then add the white chocolate pieces and stir until melted and combined. Remove from the heat and stir until almost cool, then stir in the mascarpone cheese. Pour the mixture on top of the cake and chill for 2 hours.

3 Remove the cake from the tin and transfer to a plate. Decorate the top of the cake with the caraque. Dust with cocoa powder.

double chocolate gâteau

ingredients

SERVES 10

filling

250 ml/9 fl oz whipping cream
225 g/8 oz white chocolate, broken into pieces

sponge

225 g/8 oz butter, softened, plus extra for greasing
225 g/8 oz golden caster sugar
4 eggs, beaten
175 g/6 oz self-raising flour
55 g/2 oz cocoa powder

frosting

350 g/12 oz plain chocolate, broken into pieces
115 g/4 oz butter
85 ml/3 fl oz double cream

to decorate

chocolate curls, chilled
2 tsp icing sugar and cocoa powder

method

1 To make the filling, heat the cream to almost boiling. Place the white chocolate in a food processor and chop coarsely. With the motor running, pour the cream through the feed tube. Process for 10–15 seconds, or until the mixture is smooth. Transfer to a bowl to cool, then cover and chill for 2 hours, or until firm. Whisk the mixture until just starting to hold soft peaks.

2 To make the sponge, beat the butter and sugar together until light and fluffy. Gradually beat in the eggs. Sift the flour and cocoa into another bowl, then fold into the batter. Spoon into a greased and base-lined 20-cm/8-inch deep round cake tin, level the surface, and bake in a preheated oven, 350°F/180°C, for 45–50 minutes, or until springy to the touch and the tip of a knife inserted into the centre comes out clean. Cool in the tin for 5 minutes, then cool completely on a wire rack.

3 To make the frosting, melt the chocolate. Stir in the butter and cream. Cool, stirring frequently, until the mixture is a spreading consistency. Slice the cake into 3 layers. Sandwich the layers together with the filling. Cover the cake with frosting and put chocolate curls on top. Mix together the icing sugar and cocoa and sift over the cake.

almond & hazelnut gâteau

ingredients

SERVES 8

4 eggs
100 g//3½ oz caster sugar
50 g/1¾ oz ground almonds
50 g/1¾ oz ground hazelnuts
5½ tbsp plain flour
butter, for greasing
50 g/1¾ oz flaked almonds
icing sugar, for dusting

filling

100 g/3½ oz plain chocolate
1 tbsp butter
300 ml/10 fl oz double cream

method

1 Whisk the eggs and caster sugar together for 10 minutes, or until light and foamy and the whisk leaves a trail that lasts a few seconds when lifted. Fold in the ground almonds and hazelnuts, sift the flour and fold in with a metal spoon or spatula. Pour into 2 lightly greased and base-lined 18-cm/7-inch round sandwich cake tins.

2 Sprinkle the flaked almonds over the top of one of the cakes, then bake both cakes in a preheated oven, 190°C/375°F, for 15–20 minutes, or until springy to the touch. Cool in the tins for 5 minutes, then turn out onto wire racks to cool completely.

3 To make the filling, melt the chocolate, remove from the heat, and stir in the butter. Let cool. Whip the cream until holding its shape, then fold in the chocolate until mixed.

4 Place the cake without the almond slivers on a serving plate and spread the filling over it. Leave it to set slightly, then place the almond-topped cake on top of the filling and chill in the refrigerator for 1 hour. Dust with icing sugar and serve.

double chocolate roulade

ingredients

SERVES 8

4 eggs, separated
115 g/4 oz golden caster sugar
115 g/4 oz plain chocolate, melted and cooled
1 tsp instant coffee granules, dissolved in 2 tbsp hot water, cooled
icing sugar, to decorate
cocoa powder, for dusting
fresh raspberries, to serve

filling

250 ml/9 fl oz whipping cream
140 g/5 oz white chocolate, broken into pieces
3 tbsp Tia Maria

method

1 Line a 23 x 33-cm/9 x 13-inch Swiss roll pan with nonstick baking parchment. Whisk the egg yolks and sugar in a bowl until pale and mousse-like. Fold in the chocolate, then the coffee. Place the egg whites in a clean bowl and whisk until stiff but not dry. Stir a little of the egg whites into the chocolate mixture, then fold in the remainder. Pour into the pan and bake in a preheated oven, 350°F/180°C, for 15–20 minutes, or until firm. Cover the tin with a damp tea towel and set aside for 8 hours, or overnight.

2 Meanwhile, make the filling. Heat the cream until almost boiling. Place the chocolate in a food processor and chop coarsely. With the motor running, pour the cream through the feed tube. Process until smooth. Stir in the Tia Maria. Transfer to a bowl and cool, then chill for 8 hours, or overnight.

3 To assemble the roulade, whip the chocolate cream until soft peaks form. Cut a sheet of waxed paper larger than the roulade, place on a work surface and sift icing sugar over it. Turn the roulade out onto the paper. Peel away the lining paper. Spread the chocolate cream over the roulade and roll up from the short side nearest to you. Transfer to a dish, seam-side down. Chill for 2 hours, then dust with cocoa. Serve with raspberries.

chocolate passion cake

ingredients

SERVES 6

- 5 eggs
- 150 g/5½ oz caster sugar
- 150 g/5½ oz plain flour
- 40 g/1½ oz cocoa powder
- 175 g/6 oz carrots, peeled, finely grated, and squeezed until dry
- 50 g/1¾ oz chopped walnuts
- 2 tbsp corn oil
- butter, for greasing
- 350 g/12 oz medium-fat soft cheese
- 175 g/6 oz icing sugar
- 175 g/6 oz milk or plain chocolate, melted

method

1 Place the eggs and sugar in a large bowl set over a pan of gently simmering water and, using an electric whisk, whisk until the mixture is very thick and the whisk leaves a trail that lasts a few seconds when lifted.

2 Remove the bowl from the heat. Sift the flour and cocoa into the bowl and carefully fold in. Fold in the carrots, walnuts and corn oil until the cake batter is just blended.

3 Pour into a lightly greased and base-lined 20-cm/8-inch deep round cake tin and bake in a preheated oven, 190°C/375°F, for 45 minutes. Cool slightly in the tin, then turn out onto a wire rack to cool completely.

4 Beat the soft cheese and icing sugar together until blended, then beat in the melted chocolate. Split the cake in half and sandwich together again with half the chocolate mixture. Cover the top of the cake with the remainder of the chocolate mixture, swirling it with a knife. Chill in the refrigerator or serve immediately.

chocolate & orange cake

ingredients

SERVES 8

175 g/6 oz caster sugar
175 g/6 oz butter or block margarine
3 eggs, beaten
175 g/6 oz self-raising flour, sifted
2 tbsp cocoa powder, sifted
2 tbsp milk
3 tbsp orange juice
grated rind of 1/2 orange

frosting

175 g/6 oz icing sugar
2 tbsp orange juice
a little melted chocolate

method

1 Beat the sugar and butter or margarine together in a bowl until light and fluffy. Gradually add the eggs, beating well after each addition. Carefully fold in the flour.

2 Divide the mixture in half. Add the cocoa and milk to one half, stirring until well combined. Flavour the other half with the orange juice and grated orange rind.

3 Place spoonfuls of each mixture into a lightly greased 20-cm/8-inch deep round cake tin and swirl together with a skewer, to create a marbled effect. Bake in a preheated oven, 190°C/375°F, for 25 minutes or until the cake is springy to the touch. Cool in the tin for a few minutes before transferring to a wire rack to cool completely.

4 To make the frosting, sift the icing sugar into a mixing bowl and mix in enough of the orange juice to form a smooth frosting. Spread the frosting over the top of the cake and leave to set. Pipe fine lines of melted chocolate in a decorated pattern over the top.

date & chocolate cake

ingredients

SERVES 6

115 g/4 oz plain chocolate
1 tbsp grenadine
1 tbsp golden syrup
115 g/4 oz unsalted butter plus extra for greasing
55 g/2 oz caster sugar
2 large eggs
85 g/3 oz self-raising flour plus extra for dusting
2 tbsp ground rice
1 tbsp icing sugar, to decorate

filling

115 g/4 oz dried dates, chopped
1 tbsp orange juice
1 tbsp raw sugar
25 g/1 oz blanched almonds, chopped
2 tbsp apricot jam

method

1 Break the chocolate into pieces, then place the chocolate, grenadine and syrup in the top of a double boiler or in a heatproof bowl set over a pan of barely simmering water. Stir over low heat until the chocolate has melted and the mixture is smooth. Remove the pan from the heat and set aside to cool.

2 Beat the butter and caster sugar together in a bowl until pale and fluffy. Gradually beat in the eggs, then beat in the chocolate mixture. Sift the flour into another bowl and stir in the ground rice. Fold the 2 mixtures together.

3 Divide the cake batter between 2 greased 18-cm/7-inch sandwich cake tins, dusted with flour, and level the surface. Bake in a preheated oven, 180°C/350°F, for 20–25 minutes, or until golden and firm to the touch. Turn out onto a wire rack to cool.

4 To make the filling, put all the ingredients into a saucepan and stir over low heat for 4–5 minutes, or until fully blended. Remove from the heat, allow to cool, then use the filling to sandwich the cakes together. Dust the top of the cake with icing sugar and serve.

chocolate marshmallow cake

ingredients

SERVES 6

6 tbsp unsalted butter
225 g/8 oz caster sugar
1/2 tsp vanilla essence
2 eggs, beaten lightly
85 g/3 oz plain chocolate, broken into pieces
150 ml/5 fl oz buttermilk
175 g/6 oz self-raising flour
1/2 tsp bicarbonate of soda
pinch of salt

frosting

175 g/6 oz white marshmallows
1 tbsp milk
2 egg whites
2 tbsp caster sugar

55 g/2 oz milk chocolate, grated, to decorate

method

1 Cream the butter, sugar and vanilla together in a bowl until pale and fluffy, then gradually beat in the eggs.

2 Melt the chocolate in a bowl over a saucepan of simmering water. Gradually stir in the buttermilk until well combined. Cool slightly.

3 Sift the flour, bicarbonate of soda and salt into a separate bowl. Add the chocolate and the flour mixtures alternately to the creamed mixture, a little at a time. Spoon the mixture into a 850-ml/1 1/2-pint ovenproof bowl greased with butter and smooth the surface. Bake in a preheated oven, 160°C/325°F, for 50 minutes until a skewer inserted into the centre of the cake comes out clean. Turn out onto a wire rack to cool.

4 Meanwhile, make the frosting. Heat the marshmallows and milk very gently in a small saucepan until the marshmallows have melted. Remove from the heat and cool. Whisk the egg whites until soft peaks form, then add the sugar and continue whisking, until stiff peaks form. Fold into the cooled marshmallow mixture and set aside for 10 minutes.

5 When the cake is cool, cover the top and sides with the marshmallow frosting. Top with grated milk chocolate.

family chocolate cake

ingredients

SERVES 8

125 g/4½ oz soft margarine, plus extra for greasing
125 g/4½ oz caster sugar
2 eggs
1 tbsp golden syrup
125 g/4½ oz self-raising flour, sifted
2 tbsp cocoa powder, sifted
a little milk or white chocolate, melted (optional)

filling and topping

4 tbsp icing sugar, sifted
2 tbsp butter
100 g/3½ oz white or milk cooking chocolate

method

1 Place all of the ingredients for the cake in a large mixing bowl and beat with a wooden spoon or electric mixer to form a smooth mixture.

2 Divide the mixture between 2 lightly greased 18-cm/7-inch shallow cake tins and smooth the tops. Bake in a preheated oven, 190°C/375°F, for 20 minutes or until springy to the touch. Cool for a few minutes in the tins, then transfer to a wire rack to cool completely.

3 To make the filling, beat the sugar and butter together in a bowl until light and fluffy. Melt the white or milk cooking chocolate and beat half into the icing mixture. Use the filling to sandwich the 2 cakes together.

4 Spread the remaining melted cooking chocolate over the top of the cake. Pipe circles of contrasting milk or white chocolate and feather into the cooking chocolate with a cocktail stick, if desired. Allow the cake to set before serving.

mocha cupcakes with whipped cream

ingredients

MAKES 20 CUPCAKES

2 tbsp instant espresso coffee powder
6 tbsp butter
100 g/3½ oz caster sugar
1 tbsp honey
250 ml/8 fl oz water
225 g/8 oz plain flour
2 tbsp cocoa powder
1 tsp bicarbonate of soda
3 tbsp milk
1 large egg, lightly beaten

topping

225 ml/8 fl oz whipping cream
cocoa powder, sifted, for dusting

method

1 Put 20 paper baking cases in 2 muffin tins, or put 20 double-layer paper cases on 2 baking sheets.

2 Put the coffee powder, butter, sugar, honey and water in a saucepan and heat gently, stirring, until the sugar has dissolved. Bring to the boil, then reduce the heat and simmer for 5 minutes. Pour into a large heatproof bowl and set aside to cool.

3 When the mixture has cooled, sift in the flour and cocoa. Dissolve the bicarbonate of soda in the milk, then add to the mixture with the egg and beat together until smooth. Spoon the batter into the paper cases.

4 Bake the cupcakes in a preheated oven, 180ºC/350ºF, for 15–20 minutes, or until well risen and firm to the touch. Transfer to a wire rack to cool.

5 For the topping, whisk the cream in a bowl until it holds its shape. Just before serving, spoon heaping teaspoonfuls of cream on top of each cake, then dust lightly with sifted cocoa. Store the cupcakes in the refrigerator until ready to serve.

chocolate butterfly cakes

ingredients

MAKES 12 CUPCAKES

8 tbsp soft margarine
100 g/3½ oz caster sugar
225 g/8 oz self-raising white flour
2 large eggs
2 tbsp cocoa powder
25 g/1 oz plain chocolate, melted
icing sugar, for dusting

filling

6 tbsp butter, softened
165 g/6 oz icing sugar
25 g/1 oz plain chocolate, melted

method

1 Put 12 paper baking cases in a muffin tin, or put 12 double-layer paper cases on a baking sheet.

2 Put the margarine, sugar, flour, eggs and cocoa in a large bowl and, using an electric hand whisk, beat together until just smooth. Beat in the melted chocolate. Spoon the batter into the paper cases.

3 Bake the cupcakes in a preheated oven, 180°C/350°F, for 15 minutes, or until springy to the touch. Transfer to a wire rack to cool.

4 To make the filling, put the butter in a bowl and beat until fluffy. Sift in the icing sugar and beat together until smooth. Add the melted chocolate and beat together until well mixed.

5 When the cupcakes are cold, use a serrated knife to cut a circle from the top of each cake and then cut each circle in half. Spread or pipe a little of the buttercream into the centre of each cupcake and press the 2 semicircular halves into it at an angle to resemble butterfly wings. Dust with sifted icing sugar to serve.

warm molten-centred chocolate cupcakes

ingredients

MAKES 8 CUPS

4 tbsp soft margarine
55 g/2 oz caster sugar
1 large egg
85 g/3 oz self-raising flour
1 tbsp cocoa powder
55 g/2 oz plain chocolate
icing sugar, for dusting

method

1 Put 8 paper baking cases in a muffin tin, or place 8 double-layer paper cases on a baking sheet.

2 Put the margarine, sugar, egg, flour and cocoa in a large bowl and, using an electric hand whisk, beat together until just smooth.

3 Spoon half of the batter into the paper cases. Using a teaspoon, make an indentation in the centre of each cake. Break the chocolate evenly into 8 squares and place a piece in each indentation, then spoon the remaining cake batter on top.

4 Bake the cupcakes in a preheated oven, 190°C/375°F, for 20 minutes, or until well risen and springy to the touch. Let stand for 2–3 minutes before serving warm, dusted with sifted icing sugar.

dark & white chocolate torte

ingredients

SERVES 6

4 eggs
100 g/3$^{1}/_{2}$ oz caster sugar
100 g/3$^{1}/_{2}$ oz plain flour
butter, for greasing

filling

300 ml/10 fl oz double cream
150 g/5$^{1}/_{2}$ oz plain chocolate, broken into small pieces

topping

75 g/2$^{3}/_{4}$ oz white chocolate
1 tbsp butter
1 tbsp milk
4 tbsp icing sugar

shavings of chocolate, to decorate

method

1 Whisk the eggs and caster sugar in a large bowl with an electric whisk for 10 minutes, or until the mixture is very light and foamy and the whisk leaves a trail that lasts a few seconds when lifted.

2 Sift the flour and fold in with a metal spoon or spatula. Pour into a greased and base-lined 20-cm/8-inch round springform cake tin and bake in a preheated oven, 180°C/350°F, for 35–40 minutes, or until springy to the touch. Cool slightly in the tin, then transfer to a wire rack to cool completely.

3 For the filling, place the cream in a pan and bring to the boil, stirring. Add the chocolate and stir until melted. Remove from the heat, transfer to a bowl, and leave to cool. Beat with a wooden spoon until thick.

4 Slice the cold cake horizontally into 2 layers. Sandwich the layers together with the plain chocolate cream and place on a wire rack.

5 For the topping, melt the chocolate and butter together and stir until blended. Whisk in the milk and icing sugar. Continue whisking for a few minutes until the frosting is cool. Pour it over the cake and spread with a spatula to coat the top and sides. Allow the frosting to set before serving.

chocolate brandy torte

ingredients

SERVES 12

base

250 g/9 oz gingersnaps
75 g/2¾ oz plain chocolate
100 g/3½ oz butter, plus extra for greasing

filling

225 g/8 oz plain chocolate
250 g/9 oz mascarpone cheese
2 eggs, separated
3 tbsp brandy
300 ml/10 fl oz double cream
4 tbsp caster sugar

to decorate

100 ml/3½ fl oz double cream
chocolate-covered coffee beans

method

1 Place the gingersnaps in a plastic bag and crush with a rolling pin. Transfer to a bowl. Place the chocolate and butter in a small pan and heat gently until melted, then pour over the crushed biscuits. Mix well, then press into a greased 23-cm/9-inch springform cake tin. Chill the base while preparing the filling.

2 To make the filling, place the chocolate in a heatproof bowl and set over a saucepan of simmering water, stirring, until melted. Remove from the heat and beat in the mascarpone cheese, egg yolks and brandy. Whip the cream until just holding its shape. Fold in the chocolate mixture.

3 Whisk the egg whites in a spotlessly clean, greasefree bowl until soft peaks form. Add the sugar, a little at a time, and whisk until thick and glossy. Fold into the chocolate mixture, in 2 batches, until just mixed.

4 Spoon the mixture into the prepared base and chill in the refrigerator for at least 2 hours. Carefully transfer to a serving plate. To decorate, whip the cream and pipe onto the cheesecake, add the chocolate-covered coffee beans and serve.

chocolate & almond torte

ingredients

SERVES 10

225 g/8 oz plain chocolate, broken into pieces
3 tbsp water
150 g/5½ oz brown sugar
175 g/6 oz butter, softened, plus extra for greasing
25 g/1 oz ground almonds
3 tbsp self-raising flour
5 eggs, separated
100 g/3½ oz finely chopped blanched almonds
icing sugar, for dusting
fresh berries and double cream, to serve

method

1 Melt the chocolate with the water in a saucepan set over very low heat, stirring until smooth. Add the sugar and stir until dissolved, removing the pan from the heat to prevent it overheating.

2 Add the butter in small amounts until it has melted into the chocolate. Remove from the heat and lightly stir in the ground almonds and flour. Add the egg yolks one at a time, beating well after each addition.

3 Whisk the egg whites in a large mixing bowl, until they stand in soft peaks, then fold them into the chocolate mixture with a metal spoon. Stir in the chopped almonds. Pour the mixture into a greased and base-lined 23-cm/9-inch loose-based cake tin and smooth the surface.

4 Bake in a preheated oven, 180°C/350°F, for 40–45 minutes, until well risen and firm (the cake will crack on the surface during cooking).

5 Cool in the tin for 30–40 minutes, then turn out onto a wire rack to cool completely. Dust with icing sugar and serve in slices with fresh berries and cream.

chocolate truffle torte

ingredients

SERVES 10

55 g/2 oz golden caster sugar
2 eggs
25 g/1 oz plain flour
25 g/1 oz cocoa powder, plus extra to decorate
butter, for greasing
50 ml/2 fl oz cold strong black coffee
2 tbsp brandy
icing sugar, to decorate

topping

600 ml/1 pint whipping cream
425 g/15 oz plain chocolate, melted and cooled

method

1 Place the sugar and eggs in a heatproof bowl and set over a saucepan of hot water. Whisk together until pale and mousse-like. Sift the flour and cocoa powder into a separate bowl, then fold gently into the cake batter. Pour into a greased and base-lined 23-cm/ 9-inch springform cake tin and bake in a preheated oven, 220°C/425°F, for 7–10 minutes, or until risen and firm to the touch.

2 Transfer to a wire rack to cool. Wash and dry the tin and replace the cooled cake in the tin. Mix the coffee and brandy together and brush over the cake.

3 To make the topping, place the cream in a bowl and whip until very soft peaks form. Carefully fold in the cooled chocolate. Pour the mixture over the sponge. Chill in the refrigerator for 4–5 hours, or until set.

4 To decorate the torte, sift cocoa powder over the top and remove carefully from the tin. Using strips of card or waxed paper as a guide, sift bands of icing sugar over the torte to create a striped pattern. To serve, cut into slices with a hot knife.

biscuits, bars & traybakes

This chapter seems to hold the solution to every problem – what to put in the children's lunch boxes, what to give them when they come home from school, what to offer as a gift to an aged aunt who has everything, what to make for the fund-raising cake sale, what to serve the friends who are coming for morning coffee or afternoon tea, even what to do on a rainy day.

Home-made biscuits, bars and traybakes are so much more special than bought ones, and you really can whip up a batch of your favourite recipe in almost no time. For a treat in a lunch box, go for something that includes a hint of fruit as well as chocolate, such as Apricot and Chocolate Chip Cookies or Chocolate and Apple Oaties. To give as a gift, why not try Nutty Chocolate Drizzles, Chocolate Temptations, or, at Christmas, Lebkuchen, those delicious soft, spicy cookies with an evocative aroma of the festive season. Cappuccino Squares or Mocha Brownies are the natural partner with morning coffee, and Chocolate Chip Shortbread with afternoon tea. Brownies never fail at a cake sale, and Chequerboard Biscuits are eye-catching, too.

And for that rainy day – well, what about Caramel Chocolate Shortbread? It'll really cheer you up!

nutty chocolate drizzles

ingredients

MAKES 24

- 250 g/8 oz butter or margarine, plus extra for greasing
- 325 g/11½ oz raw brown sugar
- 1 egg
- 140 g/5 oz plain flour, sifted
- 1 tsp baking powder
- 1 tsp bicarbonate of soda
- 140 g/5 oz rolled oats
- 30 g/1 oz bran
- 30 g/1 oz wheatgerm
- 85 g/3 oz mixed nuts, toasted and chopped roughly
- 175 g/6 oz plain chocolate chips
- 55 g/4 oz raisins and sultanas
- 175 g/6 oz plain chocolate, chopped roughly

method

1 In a large bowl, cream together the butter, sugar and egg. Add the flour, baking powder, bicarbonate of soda, oats, bran and wheatgerm and mix together until well combined. Stir in the nuts, chocoate chips and dried fruit.

2 Put 24 rounded tablespoonfuls of the biscuit mixture onto a large greased baking sheet. Transfer to a preheated oven, 180°C/350°F, and bake for 12 minutes, or until the biscuits are golden brown.

3 Remove the biscuits from the oven, then transfer to a wire rack to cool. While they are cooling, put the chocolate pieces into a heatproof bowl over a saucepan of gently simmering water and heat until melted. Stir the chocolate, then cool slightly. Use a spoon to drizzle the chocolate in waves over the biscuits, or spoon it into a piping nozzle and pipe zigzag lines. Store in an airtight container in the refrigerator before serving.

white chocolate biscuits

ingredients

MAKES 24

- 125 g/$4^{1}/_{2}$ oz butter, softened, plus extra for greasing
- 125 g/$4^{1}/_{2}$ oz firmly packed soft brown sugar
- 1 egg, beaten
- 200 g/7 oz self-raising flour
- pinch of salt
- 125 g/$4^{1}/_{2}$ oz white chocolate, roughly chopped
- 50 g/$1^{3}/_{4}$ oz Brazil nuts, chopped

method

1 Lightly grease several baking sheets, enough to accommodate 24 cookies. Beat the butter and sugar together in a large bowl until light and fluffy. Gradually add the beaten egg to the batter, beating well after each addition.

2 Sift the flour and salt into the batter and blend well. Stir in the white chocolate chunks and the chopped Brazil nuts.

3 Drop heaped teaspoons of the biscuit batter onto the baking sheets. Do not put more than 6 teaspoons of the batter onto each sheet as the cookies will spread during cooking.

4 Bake in a preheated oven, 190°C/375°F, for 10–12 minutes, or until just golden brown. Transfer the cookies to wire racks and leave until completely cold before serving.

chocolate butter biscuits

ingredients

MAKES ABOUT 18

100 g/3½ oz butter, softened, plus extra for greasing
100 g/3½ oz caster sugar
1 egg yolk
225 g/8 oz plain flour, sifted, plus extra for dusting
about 2 tbsp milk

icing

250 g/9 oz icing sugar, sifted
1 tbsp cocoa powder
about 3 tbsp orange juice

method

1 Put the butter and all but a tablespoon of the sugar into a large bowl and cream until pale and fluffy. Beat in the egg yolk, then add the flour and mix well. Stir in enough milk to form a smooth dough.

2 Roll out the dough on a lightly floured work surface. Cut out rounds using a 7.5-cm/3-inch biscuit cutter. Arrange the circles on 2 large, greased baking sheets, leaving enough space between them to allow them to spread during cooking. Sprinkle over the remaining sugar and bake in a preheated oven, 200°C/400°F, for 15 minutes, or until golden. Remove the biscuits from the oven, transfer to wire racks, and cool completely.

3 To make the icing, put the icing sugar and cocoa powder into a bowl. Stir in the orange juice gradually until enough has been added to make a thin icing. Put a teaspoonful of icing on each biscuit and let set before serving.

double chocolate chip cookies

ingredients

MAKES ABOUT 24

200 g/7 oz butter, softened, plus extra for greasing
200 g/7 oz golden caster sugar
1/2 tsp vanilla essence
1 large egg
225 g/8 oz plain flour
pinch of salt
1 tsp bicarbonate of soda
115 g/4 oz white chocolate chips
115 g/4 oz plain chocolate chips

method

1 Place the butter, sugar and vanilla essence in a large bowl and beat together. Gradually beat in the egg until the cookie batter is light and fluffy.

2 Sift the flour, salt and bicarbonate of soda over the cookie batter and fold in, then fold in the chocolate chips.

3 Drop dessertspoonfuls of the batter onto 2 greased baking sheets, allowing room for expansion during cooking. Bake the cookies in a preheated oven, 180°C/350°F, for 10–12 minutes, or until crisp outside but still soft inside. Cool on the baking sheets for 2 minutes, then transfer to wire racks to cool completely.

chocolate chip oaties

ingredients

MAKES ABOUT 20

115 g/4 oz butter, softened, plus extra for greasing
115 g/4 oz light brown sugar
1 egg
100 g/3½ oz rolled oats
1 tbsp milk
1 tsp vanilla essence
125 g/4½ oz plain flour
1 tbsp cocoa powder
½ tsp baking powder
175 g/6 oz plain chocolate, broken into pieces
175 g/6 oz milk chocolate, broken into pieces

method

1 Place the butter and sugar in a bowl and beat together until light and fluffy. Beat in the egg, then add the oats, milk and vanilla essence. Beat together until well blended. Sift the flour, cocoa powder and baking powder into the biscuit batter and stir. Stir in the chocolate pieces.

2 Place dessertspoonfuls of the biscuit batter on 2 greased baking sheets and flatten slightly with a fork. Bake in a preheated oven, 180°C/350°F, for 15 minutes, or until slightly risen and firm. Let cool on the baking sheets for 2 minutes, then transfer to wire racks to cool completely.

mocha walnut biscuits

ingredients

MAKES ABOUT 16

- 115 g/4 oz butter, softened, plus extra for greasing
- 115 g/4 oz light brown sugar
- 85 g/3 oz golden granulated sugar
- 1 tsp vanilla essence
- 1 tbsp instant coffee granules, dissolved in 1 tbsp hot water
- 1 egg
- 175 g/6 oz plain flour
- 1/2 tsp baking powder
- 1/4 tsp bicarbonate of soda
- 55 g/2 oz milk chocolate chips
- 55 g/2 oz shelled walnuts, roughly chopped

method

1 Place the butter, brown sugar and granulated sugar in a large mixing bowl and beat together thoroughly until light and fluffy. Place the vanilla essence, coffee and egg in a separate bowl and whisk together.

2 Gradually add the coffee mixture to the butter and sugar, beating until fluffy. Sift the flour, baking powder and bicarbonate of soda into the biscuit batter and fold in carefully. Fold in the chocolate chips and walnuts.

3 Place dessertspoonfuls of the biscuit batter onto 2 greased baking sheets, allowing room for the biscuits to spread. Bake in a preheated oven, 180°C/350°F, for 10–15 minutes, or until crisp on the outside but still soft inside. Cool on the baking sheets for 2 minutes, then transfer to wire racks to cool completely.

apricot & chocolate chip cookies

ingredients

MAKES 12–14

85 g/3 oz butter, softened, plus extra for greasing
2 tbsp golden granulated sugar
55 g/2 oz light brown sugar
1/2 tsp vanilla essence
1 egg, beaten
175 g/6 oz self-raising flour
115 g/4 oz plain chocolate, roughly chopped
115 g/4 oz no-soak dried apricots, roughly chopped

method

1 Place the butter, granulated sugar, brown sugar and vanilla essence in a bowl and beat together. Gradually beat in the egg until light and fluffy.

2 Sift the flour over the cookie batter and fold in, then fold in the chocolate and apricots.

3 Put tablespoonfuls of the cookie batter onto 2 greased baking sheets, allowing space for the cookies to spread. Bake in a preheated oven, 180°C/350°F, for 13–15 minutes, or until crisp outside but still soft inside. Cool on the baking sheets for 2 minutes, then transfer to wire racks to cool completely.

chocolate & apple oaties

ingredients

MAKES 24

115 g/4 oz apple sauce
2 tbsp apple juice
115 g/4 oz butter or margarine, plus extra for greasing
300 g/3½ oz raw brown sugar
1 tsp bicarbonate of soda
1 tsp almond essence
50 ml/2 fl oz boiling water
125 g/4½ oz rolled oats
280 g/10 oz plain flour, unsifted
pinch of salt
55 g/2 oz plain chocolate chips

method

1 Blend the apple sauce, apple juice, butter or margarine and sugar in a food processor until a fluffy consistency is reached.

2 In a separate bowl, mix together the bicarbonate of soda, almond essence and water, then add to the food processor and mix with the apple mixture. In another bowl, mix together the oats, flour and salt, then gradually stir into the apple mixture and beat well. Stir in the chocolate chips.

3 Put 24 rounded tablespoonfuls of mixture onto a large baking sheet, ensuring that they are well spaced. Transfer to a preheated oven, 200°C/400°F, and bake for 15 minutes, or until the oaties are golden brown.

4 Remove the oaties from the oven, then transfer to a wire rack and cool completely before serving.

chocolate orange biscuits

ingredients

MAKES 30

6 tbsp butter, softened

6 tbsp caster sugar

1 egg

1 tbsp milk

225 g/8 oz plain flour, plus extra for dusting

2 tbsp cocoa powder

icing

175 g/6 oz icing sugar, sifted

3 tbsp orange juice

25 g/1 oz plain chocolate, melted

method

1 Beat the butter and sugar together until light and fluffy. Beat in the egg and milk until well blended. Sift the flour and cocoa together and gradually mix together to form a soft dough. Use your fingers to incorporate the last of the flour and bring the dough together.

2 Roll out the dough on a lightly floured work surface until 5-mm/1/4-inch thick. Using a 5-cm/2-inch fluted round cutter, cut out as many biscuits as you can. Re-roll the dough trimmings and cut out more biscuits. Place the biscuits on 2 baking sheets lined with sheets of baking parchment, allowing room for expansion during cooking, and bake in a preheated oven, 180°C/350°F, for 10–12 minutes, or until golden brown.

3 Cool the biscuits on the baking sheet for a few minutes, then transfer to a wire rack and cool completely.

4 To make the icing, place the sugar in a bowl and stir in enough orange juice to form a thin icing that will coat the back of a spoon. Spread the icing over the biscuits and leave to set. Drizzle with melted chocolate and leave to set before serving.

chocolate temptations

ingredients

MAKES 24

365 g/12½ oz plain chocolate
6 tbsp unsalted butter, plus extra for greasing
1 tsp strong coffee
2 eggs
150 g/5 oz soft brown sugar
225 g/8 oz cups plain flour
¼ tsp baking powder
pinch of salt
2 tsp almond essence
50 g/1¾ oz Brazil nuts, chopped
50 g/1¾ oz hazelnuts, chopped
40 g/1½ oz white chocolate

method

1 Put 225 g/8 oz of the plain chocolate with the butter and coffee into a heatproof bowl over a saucepan of simmering water and heat until the chocolate is almost melted.

2 Meanwhile, beat the eggs in a bowl until fluffy. Whisk in the sugar gradually until thick. Remove the melted chocolate from the heat and stir until smooth, then stir it into the egg mixture until combined.

3 Sift the flour, baking powder and salt into a bowl and stir into the chocolate mixture. Chop 85 g/3 oz of plain chocolate into pieces and stir into the dough. Stir in the almond essence and nuts.

4 Put 24 rounded dessertspoonfuls of the dough on a greased baking sheet and bake in a preheated oven, 180°C/350°F, for 16 minutes. Transfer the biscuits to a wire rack to cool. To decorate, melt the remaining chocolate (plain and white) in turn, then spoon into a piping bag and pipe lines onto the biscuits.

chocolate viennese fingers

ingredients

MAKES ABOUT 30

115 g/4 oz butter, softened, plus extra for greasing

55 g/2 oz golden icing sugar, sifted

125 g/4½ oz plain flour

1 tbsp cocoa powder

100 g/3½ oz plain chocolate, melted and cooled

method

1 Beat the butter and sugar together until light and fluffy. Sift the flour and cocoa powder into the bowl and work the mixture until it is a smooth, piping consistency.

2 Spoon into a large piping bag fitted with a 2.5-cm/1-inch fluted tip. Pipe 6-cm/2½-inch lengths of the mixture onto 2 greased baking sheets, allowing room for expansion during cooking. Bake in a preheated oven, 180°C/350°F, for 15 minutes, or until firm.

3 Cool on the baking sheets for 2 minutes, then transfer to a wire rack to cool completely. Dip the ends of the biscuits into the melted chocolate and allow to set before serving.

dutch macaroons

ingredients

MAKES 20

- 2 egg whites
- 225 g/8 oz caster sugar
- 175 g/6 oz cups ground almonds
- 225 g/8 oz plain chocolate
- rice paper

method

1 Whisk the egg whites in a large, clean bowl until stiff, then fold in the sugar and ground almonds.

2 Place the mixture in a large piping bag fitted with a 1-cm/½-inch plain tip and pipe fingers, 7.5-cm/3-inches long, onto 2 baking sheets lined with rice paper, allowing room for expansion during cooking.

3 Bake in a preheated oven, 180°C/350°F, for 15–20 minutes, or until golden. Transfer to a wire rack to cool. Remove the excess rice paper from round the edges.

4 Melt the chocolate and dip the base of each macaroon into the chocolate. Place the macaroons on a sheet of baking parchment to set. Drizzle any remaining chocolate over the top of the macaroons (you may have to reheat the chocolate to do this) and set before serving.

lebkuchen

ingredients

MAKES ABOUT 60

3 eggs
200 g/7 oz golden caster sugar
55 g/2 oz plain flour
2 tsp cocoa powder
1 tsp ground cinnamon
1/2 tsp ground cardamom
1/4 tsp ground cloves
1/4 tsp ground nutmeg
175 g/6 oz ground almonds
55 g/2 oz glazed peel, finely chopped

to decorate

115 g/4 oz plain chocolate, melted and cooled
115 g/4 oz white chocolate, melted and cooled
sugar crystals

method

1 Place the eggs and sugar in a small heatproof bowl and set over a saucepan of gently simmering water. Whisk until thick and foamy. Remove the bowl from the pan and continue to whisk for 2 minutes.

2 Sift the flour, cocoa, cinnamon, cardamom, cloves and nutmeg over the egg mixture, add the ground almonds and chopped peel and stir. Drop heaped teaspoonfuls of the batter onto several baking sheets lined with baking parchment, spreading them gently into smooth mounds and allowing room for expansion during cooking.

3 Bake in a preheated oven, 160°C/325°F, for 15–20 minutes, or until light brown and slightly soft to the touch. Cool on the baking sheets for 10 minutes, then transfer to wire racks to cool completely. Dip half the biscuits in the melted plain chocolate and half in the white chocolate. Sprinkle with sugar crystals, then allow to set before serving.

chequerboard biscuits

ingredients

MAKES 18

175 g/6 oz butter, softened
6 tbsp icing sugar
1 teaspoon vanilla essence or grated rind of 1/2 orange
250 g/9 oz plain flour
25 g/1 oz plain chocolate
a little beaten egg white

method

1 Beat the butter and icing sugar in a mixing bowl until light and fluffy. Beat in the vanilla essence or grated orange rind. Gradually beat in the flour to form a soft dough. Use your fingers to incorporate the last of the flour and bring the dough together.

2 Melt the chocolate. Divide the dough in half and beat the melted chocolate into one half. Keeping each half of the dough separate, cover and chill for 30 minutes.

3 Roll out each piece of dough to a rectangle measuring 7.5 x 20 cm/3 x 8 inches and 3-cm/ 1 1/2-inches thick. Brush one piece of dough with a little egg white and place the other on top. Cut the block of dough in half lengthways and turn over one half. Brush the side of one strip with egg white and butt the other up to it, so that it resembles a chequerboard.

4 Cut the block into thin slices and place each slice flat on a lightly greased baking sheet, allowing enough room for the slices to spread out a little during cooking.

5 Bake in a preheated oven, 180°C/350°F, for about 10 minutes, until just firm. Cool the biscuits on the baking sheets for a few minutes, before transferring carefully, with a spatula, to a wire rack to cool completely.

chocolate wheatmeals

ingredients

MAKES 20

6 tbsp butter, plus extra for greasing

100 g/3½ oz raw demerara sugar

1 egg

25 g/1 oz wheat germ

125 g/4½ oz whole-wheat flour

6 tbsp self-raising flour, sifted

125 g/4½ oz chocolate

method

1 Beat the butter and sugar until fluffy. Add the egg and beat well. Stir in the wheat germ and flours. Bring the batter together with your hands.

2 Roll rounded teaspoons of the batter into balls and place on a greased baking sheet, allowing room for expansion during cooking.

3 Flatten the biscuits slightly with a fork, then bake in a preheated oven, 180°C/350°F, for 15–20 minutes, or until golden. Cool on the baking sheet for a few minutes before transferring to a wire rack to cool completely.

4 Melt the chocolate, then dip each biscuit in the chocolate to cover the bases and come a little way up the sides. Let the excess chocolate drip back into the bowl. Place the biscuits on a sheet of baking parchment and leave to set in a cool place before serving.

hazelnut bites

ingredients

MAKES 24

115 g/4 oz butter, plus extra for greasing
140 g/5 oz raw brown sugar
1 egg
1 tbsp almond essence
150 g/5 oz plain flour
3/4 tsp baking powder
pinch of salt
200 g/7 oz rolled oats
85 g/3 oz plain chocolate chips
50 g/1 3/4 oz hazelnuts, toasted and chopped
200 g/7 oz plain chocolate, chopped into small pieces

method

1 Cream the butter and sugar together in a bowl. Add the egg and almond essence and beat well. In a separate bowl, sift together the flour, baking powder and salt. Beat in the egg mixture. Stir in the oats, chocolate chips and half of the hazelnuts.

2 Put 24 rounded tablespoonfuls of the dough onto a large, greased baking sheet and flatten with a rolling pin. Transfer to a preheated oven, 180°C/350°F, and bake for 10 minutes, or until the biscuits are golden brown.

3 Remove the biscuits from the oven, then transfer to a wire rack and let them cool thoroughly. Put the chocolate pieces in a heatproof bowl over a saucepan of simmering water and heat until melted. Cover the tops of the biscuits with melted chocolate, then top with a sprinkling of the remaining hazelnuts. Cool on waxed paper then store in an airtight container in the refrigerator before serving.

chocolate chip shortbread

ingredients

SERVES 8

115 g/4 oz plain flour
55 g/2 oz cornflour
55 g/2 oz golden caster sugar
115 g/4 oz butter, diced, plus extra for greasing
40 g/1½ oz plain chocolate chips

method

1 Sift the flour and cornflour into a large mixing bowl. Stir in the sugar, then add the butter and rub it in until the mixture starts to bind together.

2 Turn into a greased 23-cm/9-inch loose-based fluted tart tin and press evenly over the base. Prick the surface with a fork. Sprinkle with the chocolate chips and press them lightly into the surface.

3 Bake the shortbread in a preheated oven, 160°C/325°F, for 35–40 minutes, or until cooked but not browned. Mark into 8 portions with a sharp knife. Cool in the tin for 10 minutes, then transfer to a wire rack to cool completely.

chocolate shortbread

ingredients

MAKES 24

350 g/12 oz plain flour, plus extra for dusting
2 tbsp cocoa powder
200 g/7 oz butter, diced, plus extra for greasing
140 g/5 oz caster sugar, plus extra for decorating
1 tbsp milk (optional)

method

1 Sift the flour and cocoa powder into a large bowl. Rub in the butter using your fingertips until the mixture resembles fine breadcrumbs. Stir in the sugar. Using your hands, shape the mixture into a firm dough. If necessary, add a little milk.

2 Roll out the dough on a lightly floured work surface to a thickness of about 1 cm/½ inch. Stamp out fancy shapes using assorted biscuit cutters about 5 cm/2 inches in diameter and 2.5 cm/1 inch deep. Alternatively, use a sharp knife to cut the dough into bars or fingers. Arrange the dough shapes on a large, greased baking sheet, leaving enough space between them to allow them to spread during cooking.

3 Bake in a preheated oven, 180°C/350°F, for 30 minutes, or until golden. Remove from the oven, transfer to a wire rack, dust with caster sugar, and cool completely.

caramel chocolate shortbread

ingredients

MAKES 24

115 g/4 oz butter, plus extra for greasing
175 g/6 oz plain flour
55 g/2 oz golden caster sugar

filling and topping

175 g/6 oz butter
115 g/4 oz golden caster sugar
3 tbsp golden syrup
400 g/14 oz canned condensed milk
200 g/7 oz plain chocolate, broken into pieces

method

1 Place the butter, flour and sugar in a food processor and process until it begins to bind together. Press the mixture into a greased and base-lined 23-cm/9-inch shallow square cake tin and smooth the top. Bake in a preheated oven, 180°C/350°F, for 20–25 minutes, or until golden.

2 Meanwhile, make the filling. Place the butter, sugar, syrup and condensed milk in a saucepan and heat gently until the sugar has melted. Bring to the boil and simmer for 6–8 minutes, stirring constantly, until the mixture becomes very thick. Pour over the shortbread base and chill in the refrigerator until firm.

3 To make the topping, melt the chocolate and leave to cool, then spread over the caramel. Chill in the refrigerator until set. Cut the shortbread into 12 pieces with a sharp knife and serve.

cappuccino squares

ingredients

MAKES 15

225 g/8 oz self-raising flour
1 tsp baking powder
1 tsp cocoa powder, plus extra for dusting
225 g/8 oz butter, softened, plus extra for greasing
225 g/8 oz golden caster sugar
4 eggs, beaten
3 tbsp instant coffee powder, dissolved in 2 tbsp hot water

white chocolate frosting

115 g/4 oz white chocolate, broken into pieces
55 g/2 oz butter, softened
3 tbsp milk
175 g/6 oz icing sugar

method

1 Sift the flour, baking powder and cocoa into a bowl and add the butter, caster sugar, eggs and coffee. Beat well, by hand or with an electric whisk, until smooth, then spoon into a greased and base-lined shallow 28 x 18-cm/ 11 x 7-inch tin and smooth the top.

2 Bake in a preheated oven, 180°C/350°F, for 35–40 minutes, or until risen and firm, then turn out onto a wire rack, peel off the lining paper, and cool completely. To make the frosting, place the chocolate, butter and milk in a bowl set over a saucepan of simmering water and stir until the chocolate has melted.

3 Remove the bowl from the pan and sift in the icing sugar. Beat until smooth, then spread over the cake. Dust the top of the cake with sifted cocoa, then cut into squares.

COLATE

chocolate fudge brownies

ingredients

MAKES 16

200 g/7 oz low-fat soft cheese
1/2 tsp vanilla essence
250 g/9 oz caster sugar
2 eggs
100 g/3 1/2 oz butter
3 tbsp cocoa powder
100 g/3 1/2 oz self-raising flour, sifted
50 g/1 3/4 oz chopped pecan nuts

fudge frosting

4 tbsp butter
1 tbsp milk
100 g/3 1/2 oz icing sugar
2 tbsp cocoa powder
pecan nuts, to decorate (optional)

method

1 Beat together the cheese, vanilla essence and 5 teaspoons of caster sugar, then set aside.

2 Beat the eggs and remaining caster sugar together until light and fluffy. Place the butter and cocoa powder in a small saucepan and heat gently, stirring until the butter melts and the mixture combines, then stir it into the egg mixture. Fold in the flour and nuts.

3 Pour half of the brownie mixture into a lightly greased 20-cm/8-inch square shallow cake tin and smooth the top. Carefully spread the soft cheese over it, then cover it with the remaining brownie mixture. Bake in a preheated oven, 180°C/350°F, for 40–45 minutes. Leave to cool in the tin.

4 To make the frosting, melt the butter in the milk. Stir in the sugar and cocoa. Using a spatula, spread the frosting over the brownies and decorate with pecan nuts (if using). Let the frosting set, then cut into squares to serve.

mocha brownies

ingredients

MAKES 16

55 g/2 oz butter, plus extra for greasing
115 g/4 oz plain chocolate, broken into pieces
175 g/6 oz brown sugar
2 eggs
1 tbsp instant coffee powder dissolved in 1 tbsp hot water, cooled
85 g/3 oz plain flour
1/2 tsp baking powder
55 g/2 oz roughly chopped pecan nuts

method

1 Place the chocolate and butter in a heavy-based saucepan over low heat until melted. Stir and set aside to cool.

2 Place the sugar and eggs in a large bowl and cream together until light and fluffy. Fold in the chocolate mixture and cooled coffee and mix thoroughly. Sift in the flour and baking powder and lightly fold into the mixture, then carefully fold in the pecan nuts.

3 Pour the batter into a greased and base-lined 20-cm/8-inch square cake tin and bake in a preheated oven, 180°C/350°F, for 25–30 minutes, or until firm and a skewer inserted into the centre comes out clean.

4 Cool in the tin for a few minutes, then run a knife round the edge of the cake to loosen it. Turn the cake out onto a wire rack, peel off the lining paper, and cool completely. When cold, cut into squares.

refrigerator cake

ingredients

MAKES 12 PIECES

55 g/2 oz raisins
2 tbsp brandy
115 g/4 oz plain chocolate, broken into pieces
115 g/4 oz milk chocolate, broken into pieces
55 g/2 oz butter, plus extra for greasing
2 tbsp corn syrup
175 g/6 oz digestive biscuits, roughly broken
55 g/2 oz flaked almonds, lightly toasted
25 g/1 oz glazed cherries, chopped

topping

100 g/3½ oz plain chocolate, broken into pieces
20 g/¾ oz butter

method

1 Place the raisins and brandy in a bowl and soak for 30 minutes. Put the chocolate, butter and syrup in a saucepan and heat gently, stirring, until melted.

2 Stir in the digestive biscuits, almonds, cherries, raisins and brandy. Turn into a greased and base-lined 18-cm/7-inch shallow square tin and let cool. Cover and chill in the refrigerator for 1 hour.

3 To make the topping, place the chocolate and butter in a small heatproof bowl and melt over a saucepan of gently simmering water. Stir and pour the chocolate mixture over the biscuit base. Chill in the refrigerator for 8 hours, or overnight. Cut into bars or squares to serve.

chocolates & petits fours

This is where you really stray into chocolate paradise with some fabulous recipes. If you've ever gazed into the window of a chocolate shop and sighed wistfully, wishing you could try one of everything, here is your chance! Light, fluffy truffles, sophisticated chocolate liqueurs, rich, buttery fudge, wafer-thin Florentines, and the aptly named Rocky Road Bites, hidden lumps and bumps of marshmallows, walnuts and apricots – they are all here for you to make. Some you will want to share with your family and friends, and some you might want to save for yourself!

Chocolates and petits fours are a great way to round off a special occasion meal, especially those that have a little liqueur added. Irish Cream Truffles, Italian Chocolate Truffles, Rum Truffles, Chocolate Orange Collettes, Chocolate Liqueurs and Rum and Chocolate Cups will all go down well with after-dinner coffee. For family parties and festive occasions, try the fudge recipes, Brazil Nut Brittle, Nutty Chocolate Clusters and of course those Rocky Road Bites. For a really special, thoughtful gift, the Chocolate Mascarpone Cups, Mini Chocolate Cones, Ladies' Kisses, Mini Florentines and Chocolate Biscotti look particularly attractive packaged in a pretty box.

And as a treat for yourself? Well, that's up to you!

white chocolate & pistachio truffles

ingredients

MAKES 26–30

100 g/3½ oz white chocolate, broken into pieces

15 g/½ oz butter

75 ml/2½ fl oz double cream

25 g/1 oz shelled unsalted pistachios, finely chopped

icing sugar, for coating

method

1 Place the chocolate, butter and cream in a heatproof bowl and set over a pan of gently simmering water until melted, without stirring. Remove the bowl from the heat and stir gently, then stir in the nuts. Cool, then cover with clingfilm and chill in the refrigerator for 8 hours, or overnight.

2 Line a baking sheet with nonstick baking parchment. Take teaspoonfuls of the mixture and roll into balls. Place the truffles on the prepared baking sheet and chill for 2 hours, or until firm.

3 Just before serving, roll the truffles in icing sugar to coat.

white chocolate truffles

ingredients

MAKES 12

2 tbsp unsalted butter

5 tbsp double cream

225 g/8 oz good-quality Swiss white chocolate

1 tbsp orange-flavoured liqueur (optional)

to finish

100 g/3½ oz white chocolate

method

1 Line a Swiss roll tin with a sheet of baking parchment.

2 Place the butter and cream in a small saucepan and bring slowly to the boil, stirring constantly. Boil the mixture for 1 minute, then remove the pan from the heat.

3 Break the chocolate into pieces and add to the cream. Stir until melted, then beat in the orange-flavoured liqueur (if using). Pour into the prepared tin and chill for about 2 hours, until firm.

4 Break off pieces of the truffle mixture and roll them into balls. Chill for a further 30 minutes before finishing the truffles.

5 To finish, melt the white chocolate in a bowl set over a saucepan of gently simmering water. Dip the balls in the chocolate, allowing the excess to drip back into the bowl. Place on nonstick baking parchment, swirl the chocolate with the tines of a fork, and leave to harden.

irish cream truffles

ingredients

MAKES ABOUT 24

150 ml/5 fl oz double cream
225 g/8 oz plain chocolate, broken into pieces
25 g/1 oz butter
3 tbsp Irish cream liqueur
115 g/4 oz white chocolate, broken into pieces
115 g/4 oz plain chocolate, broken into pieces

method

1 Heat the cream in a saucepan over low heat but do not let it boil. Remove from the heat and stir in the chocolate and butter. Stand for 2 minutes, then stir until smooth. Stir in the liqueur. Pour the mixture into a bowl and cool. Cover with clingfilm and chill in the refrigerator for 8 hours, or overnight, until firm.

2 Line a baking sheet with nonstick baking parchment. Take teaspoonfuls of the chilled chocolate mixture and roll into small balls. Place the balls on the prepared baking sheet and chill in the refrigerator for 2–4 hours, or until firm. Melt the white chocolate pieces and cool slightly.

3 Coat half the truffles by spearing on thin skewers or cocktail sticks and dipping into the white chocolate. Transfer to a sheet of nonstick baking parchment to set. Melt the plain chocolate and cool slightly, then use to coat the remaining truffles in the same way. Store the truffles in the refrigerator in an airtight container, separated by layers of waxed paper, for up to 1 week.

italian chocolate truffles

ingredients

MAKES 24

175 g/6 oz plain chocolate
2 tbsp Amaretto liqueur or orange-flavoured liqueur
3 tbsp unsalted butter
4 tbsp icing sugar
50 g/1¾ oz ground almonds
50 g/1¾ oz grated chocolate

method

1 Melt the plain chocolate with the liqueur in a bowl set over a saucepan of hot water, stirring until well combined.

2 Add the butter and stir until it has melted. Stir in the icing sugar and the ground almonds. Leave the mixture in a cool place until it is firm enough to roll into 24 balls.

3 Place the grated chocolate on a plate and roll the truffles in the chocolate to coat them. Place in paper petit four cases and chill.

rum truffles

ingredients

MAKES 12

125 g/5 1/2 oz plain chocolate
small piece of butter
2 tbsp rum
50 g/1 3/4 oz shredded coconut
100 g/3 1/2 oz cake crumbs
6 tbsp icing sugar
2 tbsp cocoa powder

method

1 Break the chocolate into pieces and place in a bowl with the butter. Set the bowl over a saucepan of gently simmering water and stir until melted and combined.

2 Remove from the heat and beat in the rum. Stir in the shredded coconut, cake crumbs and two-thirds of the icing sugar. Beat until combined. Add a little extra rum if the mixture is stiff.

3 Roll the mixture into small balls and place them on a sheet of baking parchment. Chill until firm.

4 Sieve the remaining icing sugar onto a large plate. Sieve the cocoa powder onto another plate. Roll half of the truffles in the icing sugar until thoroughly coated and roll the remaining rum truffles in the cocoa.

5 Place the truffles in paper petit four cases and chill in the refrigerator.

chocolate orange collettes

ingredients

MAKES 20

280 g/10 oz plain chocolate, broken into pieces
1/2 tsp corn oil
150 ml/5 fl oz double cream
finely grated rind of 1/2 orange
1 tbsp Cointreau

to decorate

chopped nuts
fine strips of orange rind

method

1 Melt 150 g/5 1/2 oz of the chocolate with the oil and stir until mixed. Spread evenly over the inside of 20 double petit four cases, taking care to keep a good thickness round the edge. Chill for 1 hour, or until set, then apply a second coat of chocolate, remelting if necessary. Chill for 1 hour, or until set.

2 Place the cream and grated orange rind in a saucepan and heat until almost boiling. Remove from the heat, add the remaining chocolate pieces and stir until smooth. Return to the heat and stir until the mixture starts to bubble. Remove from the heat and stir in the Cointreau, then cool. Peel the paper cases off the chocolate cups.

3 Beat the chocolate cream until thick, then spoon into a large piping bag fitted with a fluted tip. Pipe the chocolate cream into the chocolate cases. Decorate some of the chocolate collettes with chopped nuts and some with a few strips of orange rind. Cover and keep in the refrigerator. Use within 2–3 days.

chocolate liqueurs

ingredients

MAKES 40

100 g/3½ oz plain chocolate
5 glacé cherries, halved
10 hazelnuts or macadamia nuts
150 ml/5 fl oz double cream
2 tbsp icing sugar
4 tbsp liqueur

to finish

50 g/1¾ oz plain chocolate, melted
a little white chocolate, melted, or white chocolate curls, or extra nuts and cherries

method

1 Line a baking sheet with a sheet of baking parchment. Break the plain chocolate into pieces, place in a bowl and set over a saucepan of hot water. Stir until melted. Spoon the chocolate into 20 paper petit four cases, spreading up the sides with a small spoon or brush. Place upside down on the baking sheet and leave to set.

2 Carefully peel away the paper cases. Place a cherry or nut in the bottom of each cup.

3 To make the filling, place the double cream in a mixing bowl and sift the icing sugar on top. Whisk the cream until it is just holding its shape, then whisk in the liqueur to flavour it.

4 Place the cream in a piping bag fitted with a 1-cm/½-inch plain tip and pipe a little into each chocolate case. Chill for 20 minutes.

5 To finish, spoon the plain chocolate over the cream to cover it and pipe the melted white chocolate on top, swirling it into the plain chocolate with a cocktail stick. Set aside to harden. Alternatively, cover the cream with the melted plain chocolate and decorate with white chocolate curls before setting. If you prefer, place a small piece of nut or cherry on top of the cream, then cover with plain chocolate.

chocolate marzipans

ingredients

MAKES 30

450 g/1 lb marzipan
25 g/1 oz glacé cherries, very finely chopped
icing sugar, for dusting
25 g/1 oz stem ginger, very finely chopped
50 g/1¾ oz no-soak dried apricots, very finely chopped
350 g/12 oz plain chocolate, broken into pieces
25 g/1 oz white chocolate

method

1 Line a baking sheet with nonstick baking parchment. Divide the marzipan into 3 balls and knead each ball to soften it.

2 Work the glacé cherries into 1 portion of the marzipan by kneading on a work surface lightly dusted with icing sugar. Do the same with the stem ginger and another portion of marzipan, then the apricots and the third portion of marzipan. Form each flavoured portion of marzipan into small balls, keeping the flavours separate.

3 Place the plain chocolate in a heatproof bowl and set over a saucepan of hot water. Stir until the chocolate has melted. Dip one ball of marzipan of each flavour into the melted chocolate by spiking each one with a cocktail stick, allowing the excess chocolate to drip back into the bowl.

4 Place the balls of the 3 flavours in clusters on the baking sheet. Repeat with the remaining balls. Chill in the refrigerator for 1 hour, or until set. Place the white chocolate in a small heatproof bowl and set over a saucepan of simmering water. Stir until the chocolate has melted. Drizzle a little over the tops of each cluster of marzipan balls. Chill in the refrigerator for 1 hour, or until hard. Remove from the baking parchment, arrange on a plate and serve.

chocolate mascarpone cups

ingredients

MAKES 20

100 g/3$^1/_2$ oz plain chocolate

filling

100 g/3$^1/_2$ oz milk or plain chocolate

200 g/7 oz mascarpone cheese

cocoa powder, for dusting

$^1/_4$ tsp vanilla essence

method

1 Line a baking sheet with a sheet of baking parchment. Break the plain chocolate into pieces, place in a bowl and set over a saucepan of hot water. Stir until melted. Spoon the chocolate into 20 paper petit four cases, spreading up the sides with a small spoon or brush. Place the chocolate cups upside down on the baking sheet and let set. When set, carefully peel away the paper cases.

2 To make the filling, melt the chocolate. Place the mascarpone cheese in a bowl and beat in the vanilla essence and melted chocolate until well combined. Chill the mixture in the refrigerator, beating occasionally until firm enough to pipe.

3 Place the mascarpone filling in a piping bag fitted with a star tip and pipe the mixture into the cups. Decorate with a dusting of cocoa.

mini chocolate cones

ingredients

MAKES 10

75 g/2¾ oz plain chocolate
100 ml/3½ fl oz double cream
1 tbsp icing sugar
1 tbsp crème de menthe
chocolate-covered coffee beans, to decorate (optional)

method

1 Cut 10 x 7.5-cm/3-inch circles of baking parchment. Shape each circle into a cone shape and secure with a piece of sticky tape.

2 Break the chocolate into pieces, place in a heatproof bowl and set over a pan of hot water. Stir until the chocolate has melted. Using a small pastry brush or clean artist's brush, brush the inside of each cone with the melted chocolate.

3 Brush a second layer of chocolate on the inside of the cones and chill in the refrigerator for 2 hours, or until set. Carefully peel away the paper.

4 Place the cream, icing sugar and crème de menthe in a large bowl and whip until just holding its shape. Place in a piping bag fitted with a star tip and pipe the mixture into the chocolate cones. Decorate the cones with chocolate-covered coffee beans, if using, and chill in the refrigerator for 1–2 hours.

rum & chocolate cups

ingredients

SERVES 12

55 g/2 oz plain chocolate, broken into pieces

12 toasted hazelnuts

filling

115 g/4 oz plain chocolate, broken into pieces

1 tbsp dark rum

4 tbsp mascarpone cheese

method

1 To make the chocolate cups, place the plain chocolate in the top of a double boiler or in a heatproof bowl set over a pan of barely simmering water. Stir over low heat until the chocolate is just melted but not too runny, then remove from the heat. Spoon 1/2 teaspoon of melted chocolate into a foil confectionery case and brush it over the base and up the sides. Coat 11 more foil cases in the same way and set for 30 minutes. Chill in the refrigerator for 15 minutes. If necessary, reheat the chocolate in the double boiler or heatproof bowl to melt it again, then coat the foil cases with a second, slightly thinner coating. Chill in the refrigerator for a further 30 minutes.

2 To make the filling, place the chocolate in the top of a double boiler or in a heatproof bowl set over a saucepan of barely simmering water. Stir over low heat until melted and smooth, then remove from the heat. Cool slightly, stir in the rum and beat in the mascarpone cheese until smooth. Cool completely, stirring occasionally.

3 Spoon the filling into a piping bag fitted with a 1-cm/1/2-inch star tip. Carefully peel away the confectionery cases from the chocolate cups. Pipe the filling into the cups and top each one with a toasted hazelnut.

easy chocolate fudge

ingredients

MAKES 25 PIECES

75 g/2 3/4 oz unsalted butter, cut into even-size pieces, plus extra for greasing
500 g/1 lb 2 oz plain chocolate
400 g/14 oz canned sweetened condensed milk
1/2 tsp vanilla essence

method

1 Lightly grease a 20-cm/8-inch square cake tin with butter. Break the chocolate into small pieces and place in a large, heavy-based saucepan with the butter and condensed milk.

2 Heat gently, stirring constantly, until the chocolate and butter melt and the mixture is smooth. Do not let boil. Remove from the heat. Beat in the vanilla essence, then beat the mixture for a few minutes until thickened. Pour it into the tin and level the top.

3 Chill the mixture in the refrigerator for 1 hour, or until firm. Tip the fudge out onto a cutting board and cut into squares to serve.

pecan mocha fudge

ingredients

MAKES 80 PIECES

300 ml/10 fl oz milk
1 kg/2 lb 4 oz golden granulated sugar
250 g/9 oz butter, plus extra for greasing
2 tbsp instant coffee granules
2 tbsp cocoa powder
2 tbsp golden syrup
400 g/14 oz canned condensed milk
115 g/4 oz shelled pecan nuts, chopped

method

1 Grease a 30 x 23-cm/12 x 9-inch Swiss roll tin. Place the milk, sugar and butter in a large saucepan. Stir over gentle heat until the sugar has dissolved. Stir in the coffee granules, cocoa, syrup and condensed milk.

2 Bring to the boil and boil steadily, whisking constantly, for 10 minutes, or until a temperature of 116°C/241°F has been reached on a sugar thermometer, or a small amount of the mixture forms a soft ball when dropped into cold water.

3 Cool for 5 minutes, then beat vigorously with a wooden spoon until the mixture starts to thicken. Stir in the nuts. Continue beating until the mixture takes on a fudge-like consistency. Quickly pour into the prepared tin and stand in a cool place to set. Cut the fudge into squares to serve.

rocky road bites

ingredients

MAKES 18

125 g/5 1/2 oz milk chocolate
50 g/1 3/4 oz mini multi-coloured marshmallows
25 g/1 oz chopped walnuts
25 g/1 oz no-soak dried apricots, chopped

method

1 Line a baking sheet with baking parchment and set aside.

2 Break the chocolate into small pieces and place in a large mixing bowl. Set the bowl over a pan of simmering water and stir until the chocolate has melted. Stir in the marshmallows, walnuts and apricots, and toss in the melted chocolate until well covered.

3 Place heaping teaspoons of the mixture onto the prepared baking sheet. Chill in the refrigerator until set, then carefully remove from the baking parchment. Place in paper petit four cases to serve, if wished.

brazil nut brittle

ingredients

MAKES 20

oil, for brushing
350 g/12 oz plain chocolate, broken into pieces
85 g/3 oz shelled Brazil nuts, chopped
175 g/6 oz white chocolate, coarsely chopped
175 g/6 oz fudge, roughly chopped

method

1 Brush the bottom of a 20-cm/8-inch square cake tin with oil and line with baking parchment. Melt half the plain chocolate and spread in the prepared tin.

2 Sprinkle with the chopped Brazil nuts, white chocolate and fudge. Melt the remaining plain chocolate pieces and pour over the top.

3 Leave the brittle to set, then break up into jagged pieces using the tip of a strong knife.

nutty chocolate clusters

ingredients

MAKES 30

175 g/6 oz white chocolate

100 g/3½ oz digestive biscuits

100 g/3½ oz chopped macadamia nuts or brazil nuts

25 g/1 oz stem ginger, chopped (optional)

175 g/6 oz plain chocolate

method

1 Line a baking sheet with a sheet of baking parchment. Break the white chocolate into small pieces and melt in a mixing bowl set over a saucepan of gently simmering water.

2 Break the digestive biscuits into small pieces. Stir the biscuits into the melted chocolate with the chopped nuts and stem ginger (if using).

3 Place heaped teaspoons of the chocolate cluster mixture onto the prepared baking sheet. Chill until set, then carefully remove from the baking parchment.

4 Melt the plain chocolate and cool slightly. Dip the clusters into the chocolate, letting the excess drip back into the bowl. Return to the baking sheet and chill until set.

apricot & almond clusters

ingredients

MAKES 24–28

115 g/4 oz plain chocolate, broken into pieces
2 tbsp honey
115 g/4 oz no-soak dried apricots, chopped
55 g/2 oz blanched almonds, chopped

method

1 Place the chocolate and honey in a bowl and set over a saucepan of gently simmering water until the chocolate has melted. Stir in the apricots and almonds.

2 Drop teaspoonfuls of the mixture into petit four cases. Let set for 2–4 hours, or until firm.

chocolate cherries

ingredients

MAKES 24

12 glacé cherries
2 tbsp rum or brandy
250 g/9 oz marzipan
125 g/5½ oz plain chocolate
extra milk, plain or white chocolate, to decorate (optional)

method

1 Line a baking sheet with a sheet of baking parchment.

2 Cut the glacé cherries in half and place in a small bowl. Add the rum or brandy and stir to coat. Let the cherries soak for at least 1 hour, stirring occasionally.

3 Divide the marzipan into 24 pieces and roll each piece into a ball. Press half a cherry into the top of each marzipan ball.

4 Break the chocolate into pieces, place in a bowl, and set over a saucepan of hot water. Stir until melted. Dip each marzipan ball into the melted chocolate using a toothpick, allowing the excess to drip back into the bowl. Place the coated cherries on the baking parchment and chill until set.

5 If wished, melt a little extra chocolate and drizzle it over the top of the coated cherries. Set aside until set.

ladies' kisses

ingredients

MAKES 20

140 g/5 oz unsalted butter
115 g/4 oz caster sugar
1 egg yolk
115 g/4 oz ground almonds
175 g/6 oz plain flour
55 g/2 oz plain chocolate, broken into pieces
2 tbsp icing sugar
2 tbsp cocoa powder

method

1 Beat the butter and sugar together in a bowl until pale and fluffy. Beat in the egg yolk, then beat in the almonds and flour. Continue beating until well mixed. Shape the dough into a ball, wrap in clingfilm and chill in the refrigerator for 1½–2 hours.

2 Unwrap the dough, break off walnut-size pieces, and roll them into balls between the palms of your hands. Place the dough balls on 3 baking sheets lined with baking parchment, allowing room for expansion during cooking. Bake in a preheated oven, 160°C/325°F, for 20–25 minutes, or until golden brown. Carefully transfer the biscuits, still on the baking parchment, to wire racks to cool.

3 Place the plain chocolate in a small heatproof bowl and set over a saucepan of barely simmering water, stirring constantly, until melted. Remove from the heat.

4 Remove the biscuits from the baking parchment, and spread the melted chocolate over the bases. Sandwich them together in pairs and return to the wire racks to cool. Dust with a mixture of icing sugar and cocoa powder and serve.

mini florentines

ingredients

MAKES 40

85 g/3 oz butter, plus extra for greasing
75 g/2¾ oz caster sugar
2 tbsp sultanas or raisins
2 tbsp chopped glacé cherries
2 tbsp chopped crystallized ginger
25 g/1 oz sunflower seeds
100 g/3½ oz flaked almonds
2 tbsp double cream
175 g/6 oz plain chocolate

method

1 Grease and flour 2 baking sheets or line with baking parchment.

2 Gently heat the butter in a small saucepan until melted. Add the sugar, stir until dissolved, then bring the mixture to the boil. Remove from the heat and stir in the sultanas or raisins, cherries, ginger, sunflower seeds and almonds. Mix well, then beat in the cream.

3 Place small teaspoons of the fruit and nut mixture onto the prepared baking sheet, allowing plenty of space for the mixture to spread. Bake in a preheated oven, 180°C/350°F, for 10–12 minutes or until light golden in colour.

4 Remove from the oven and, while still hot, use a circular biscuit cutter to pull in the edges to form perfect circles. Let cool and go crisp before removing from the baking sheet.

5 Break the chocolate into pieces, place in a bowl over a saucepan of hot water and stir until melted. Spread most of the chocolate onto a sheet of baking parchment. When the chocolate is on the point of setting, carefully place the florentines flat-side down on the chocolate and leave to harden completely.

6 Cut around the florentines and remove from the baking parchment. Spread a little more chocolate on the coated side of the florentines and use a fork to mark waves in the chocolate. Leave to set and keep cool.

chocolate biscotti

ingredients

MAKES 16

1 egg
100 g/3½ oz caster sugar
1 tsp vanilla essence
125 g/5½ oz plain flour
½ tsp baking powder
1 tsp ground cinnamon
50 g/1¾ oz plain chocolate, chopped roughly
50 g/1¾ oz toasted flaked almonds
50 g/1¾ oz pine nuts
butter, for greasing

method

1 Whisk the egg, sugar and vanilla essence in a mixing bowl with an electric mixer until thick and pale – ribbons of mixture should trail from the whisk as you lift it.

2 Sift the flour, baking powder and cinnamon into a separate bowl, then sift into the egg mixture and fold in gently. Stir in the chopped plain chocolate, toasted flaked almonds and pine nuts.

3 Turn out onto a lightly floured work surface and shape into a flat log, 23 cm/9 inches long and 1.5 cm/¾ inch wide. Transfer to a large, lightly greased baking sheet.

4 Bake in a preheated oven, 180°C/350°F, for 20–25 minutes or until golden. Remove the log from the oven and cool for 5 minutes or until firm.

5 Transfer the log to a cutting board. Using a serrated bread knife, cut the log on the diagonal into slices about 1 cm/½ inch thick and arrange them on the baking sheet. Cook for 10–15 minutes, turning halfway through the cooking time.

6 Cool for 5 minutes on the baking sheet, then transfer to a wire rack to cool completely.